Closer Together

Text Alexander Ståhle
Commissioning editor Tobias Barenthin Lindblad
Design, cover art and illustrations Martin Ander
Illustrations pp 142-147 by Linda Sofie Bäckstedt
Translation Katarina Trodden

This book is published with support from FOR-
MAS and KTH.

Dokument Press
Box 773
120 02 Årsta

info@dokument.org
dokument.org

Alexander Ståhle

CLOSER TOGETHER

This Is the Future Of Cities

DOKUMENT
PRESS

Contents

Preface

Even when I am standing on a path in the middle of the woods I am sometimes struck by the thought, "What if they were to develop this place ... What would it look like?" After all, unless development increases density in the city, they will have to build out here because of the housing shortage. Considering the traffic situation in central Stockholm I can understand that people will want to move further out, especially families with children.

This is the urban researcher's fundamental dilemma; it is always on my mind. I am always working, every single minute of the day, no matter where I am in the world. As I am standing in the middle of the city centre with my two children and my bags of shopping I instead find myself wondering what the street I am standing on would have looked like if it had been built for people instead of cars. Why is it not possible to let go of the kids and allow them to move around on their own? How did this all come about? Could it be different?

"Take three large spoonfuls," said the man and handed over a glass jar filled with some kind of finely ground spice. He told me it was cumin. "Wash it down with three large glasses of water and you will feel a lot better." I had spent two days walking around the labyrinthine, narrow, medieval, crowded commercial district of Marrakech. The intense commerce in the pedestrian souk was accompanied by my, to put it mildly, unsettled stomach. It was an intensely bewildering experience that engaged all my senses and made me think of how cities used to be. Did Swedish town centres look like this only a hundred years ago? I was suddenly able to understand how frustrated the modernist architects must have felt, what with the chaos and the many downsides of the pre-modern cityscape, the brutal commercialism and the unhealthy atmosphere. The idea of giving every citizen access to new, clean housing, bathed in daylight and overlooking lush parks with workplaces and services only a few minutes away by car must of course have appeared quite extraordinary and irresistible to politicians and developers at the time. This vision became very much a reality in the Western world during the course of the 20th century, and more recently in the rest of the world.

A small, dark restaurant in central Osaka springs to mind. I was sitting in a dark, secluded space together with some other people. We were served sushi and various small dishes. Something new turned up on the table; it tasted different, kind of chewy. I asked what it was and I was told it was raw chicken! Oh my God, I thought to myself, and my mother's salmonella mantra began to play on a loop inside my head. I was to perform at a house club afterwards, and since this was my first gig on my tour of Japan I was already feeling nervous. Five hours later I was on stage in an old, black warehouse underneath a throbbing metro track looking out over five hundred jumping club kids. My stomach was calm, but my heart was racing.

The first time I was asked about my stage name, Stockholm Cyclo, was during an interview for a Japanese house magazine. "I cycle around Stockholm a lot," I replied. Cyclo means cycle taxi in South-East Asia, and I thought it was a suitable name since I always moved around town on my bike at the time – I still do. I wanted to bring the listeners on a journey via my music, but music has also allowed me to do my own travelling. Modern information technology and the Internet allow anyone to produce and disseminate music freely. It has revolutionised modern dance music, and it has made countless international contacts possible. Wherever I went – Tokyo, New York, Milan or St. Petersburg – there was a local club scene that catered to my own type of house music. It was an urban network, a small global movement that was thriving in city basements and dim-lit clubs.

Noah Raford was a house DJ based in San Francisco. We met for the first time at a conference on urban analysis in London in 2003. We were both young, keen urban scholars, and we shared a great interest in electronic dance music. This was the beginning of our friendship and close collaboration. In 2012, we received a grant from the Swedish Research Council FORMAS, which allowed us to embark on our dream project, Post Car(d) Urbanism. This project has taught me a lot about futurology and I have been able to systematically observe the visions and trends of our time over the course of four years. This book summarizes the Post Car(d) Urbanism project.

Our field of research has primarily been concerned with cities in Sweden, but this book is just as much about what is going on in the United States and Europe, which is strongly reflected across the rest of the world. The United States is especially well represented since there is a very interesting ongoing debate within the American research and planning community on how to plan for the cities and traffic of the future.

"You can't predict the future. It doesn't matter how much research we do, we can never predict what will happen." This is a common remark in discussions about futurology. Sure, some things are outside of our control, the world is a big and complex place, but we are now faced with the result of the ideas and models urban architects and engineers back in the 1920s made of the city – Car City – they envisioned for the future. They showed that the way they saw the future could become a reality if only the conditions were right, but they were not able to predict everything; urban sprawl and road construction projects have in fact brought people further apart. We have been forced to become dependent on cars. Car City did not turn out to be as attractive as the modernists hoped. It is no longer a sustainable solution. We must now build new and better future scenarios, and this is where futurologists come in.

This is a book about why and how a different kind of city can, and probably will, become a reality; a more equal, attractive, climate aware, child friendly and cleaner city; a city with a great many buildings, streets and parks; a city where the centre is not in conflict with the suburbs; a city in which children can play in the streets and where the older generation can watch them grow up; a city in which people with different incomes and backgrounds come together in a public space worth it's name; a city where emotional proximity and trust can grow. I am not talking about an ideal city, a utopia, but a multitude of widely different cities of every description. That is why this book is more about urbanisation, the urban environment and traffic and less about construction, buildings and architecture.

I wrote this book in order to show how and why change is possible and that major changes are already underway. Many politicians, developers and citizens are pushing developments in this direction because closeness is the ultimate goal of the city. Everyone in the city has a right to closeness. That is the subject of this book.

Acknowledgements

The following people have been indispensable as discussion partners and for offering support and encouragement:

Noah Raford drew up the outlines for the research project on which this book is based. It was made possible through funding from the Swedish Research Council FORMAS. Wendy Schultz of Infinite Futures, who built scenarios and wrote the report, and Daniel Jonsson at The Royal Institute of Technology (KTH), who modelled the scenarios and carried out traffic analyses, have also made major contributions to this project. Architect Linda Sofie Bäckstedt at the Royal Institute of Technology made the amazing photomontages that were published in the national daily *Dagens Nyheter*.

One major event that took place during the course of the Post Car(d) Urbanism project was the Citymoves conference, held in Stockholm in May, 2015, at the initiative of Karin Lundgren of the Royal Institute of Technology who was also head of the conference. More than four hundred people visited the Södra Teatern event, which was generously supported by contributions from the City of Stockholm and several construction companies. Five popup parks and twenty workshops took place during the conference. Participants were guided around different streets and locations while discussing the future of cities. Janette Sadik-Khan, former commissioner of the New York City Department for Transportation, was the keynote speaker. She made a great impression on the participants as well as on politicians and planners from the Stockholm city council that she met with.

I would especially like to thank Janette for the commitment and inspiration that she and her team at NACTO and Bloomberg Associates have contributed to my work on this book. Other important contributors in the United States are Jeff Wood of The Overhead Wire, Caroline Samponaro of Transportation Alternatives, Charles Montgomery of Happy City, Mike Lydon of Street Plans Collaborative, Tim Tompkins of Times Square Alliance and Ethan Kent of Project for Public Spaces. In Sweden, the grassroots organisations Alternativ Stad, Planka.nu, Urbanisma, Happy Sweden and Pennypodden have offered much inspiration. I have had the pleasure of meeting the Mayor of Bogotá, Enrique Peñalosa, on several occasions, and it will become clear to you as you read this book how impressed I am by his vision and determination. Janette and Enrique are perhaps the brightest shining stars in this field right now.

The years I spent at the KTH School of Architecture and working at the Spatial Analys och Design research centre have been especially important, and I give special credit to my mentor and director of research, Lars Marcus, who started the company Spacescape that I have led since 2008. My discussions with Lars have been long, tough and fun. Together with my amazing colleagues at Spacescape – Tobias Nordström, Malin Dahlhielm, Staffan Swartz, Helena Lundin Kleberg, Joel Hernbäck, Ida Wezelius and Linda Kummel – I have had the opportunity to participate in some major, fascinating urban development projects such as Nya Slussen, Vision City, Bostadspotential Stockholm, Värdering av stadskvalitet, Älvstaden,

Oslo Cykelstrategi and Nya Kiruna to mention but a few. They have kept me grounded while adding relevance and urgency to my research. This hands-on approach has put me in contact with many wonderful people who have dedicated their lives to making cities better places: Anders Sandberg, Niklas Svensson, Anna Forsberg, Katarina Borg, Paul Alarcon, Krister Lindstedt, Peter Granström, Staffan Claesson and Björn Siesjö are some of the internal activists I have had the pleasure of working with. I would like to extend a special thanks to Daniel Firth of the Stockholm Traffic Department, Claes Caldenby of Chalmers University of Technology, Tobias Nordström and Eva Minoura of Spacescape, and Anders Gullberg, Johannes Gustavsson and Karin Lundgren of the Royal Institute of Technology who have read and commented on my manuscript.

I would also like to thank Tobias Barenthin Lindblad at Dokument Press for his commitment and attention to detail and to Sara Johansson, who has been a passionate and critical sparring partner. There is no one I am more comfortable with when it comes to discussing urban planning, politics and ethics. Finally, I would like to thank my beloved parents who have always read my work and discussed it with me, and who have always supported me in life.

This book is dedicated to my daughters Hanna and Karin.

HOW DID WE END UP HERE?

Powerful images of the city

Hundreds of people are running in panic towards the space-craft. They are escaping from a dirty, unsafe, crowded, chaotic city in the hope of reaching Elysium, a space station to which wealthy citizens have moved after the earth has been destroyed and the cities turned into slums. In the film *Elysium* – named for the paradise of ancient Greece – this is a place described as a perfect, green, undulating park where a lucky few are living in temple-like garden communities.

The post-apocalyptic city looks good on the big screen. *War of the Worlds, The Day After Tomorrow, I Am Legend, World War Z* and *Bladerunner* are but a few examples. The hero is usually rescued and brought to a brighter, greener place in some kind of vehicle, often a car. After a seemingly endless series of car chases, the fifth biggest blockbuster of all time, *Fast and Furious 7*, ends with a scene that shows a happily united family on a beautiful beach.[1] Their car has helped them achieve a life of joy and freedom. The escape can also be portrayed in more subtle ways as in the Pixar movie *Up* in which an elderly man finds his home surrounded by a brutal, expanding city. With the help of a small boy he moves the entire house to a mountaintop in the Amazon where he finds happiness in the end.

This brave new world can also be seductively portrayed, as in *Barbie – Life in the Dreamhouse* in which all social interaction takes place in and around a gigantic pink McMansion.[2] This is a predictable, sparkling world that even my own children find irresistible. Life in *The Simpsons* and *Family Guy*, both of which portray the American dream, is equally predictable. The toy world in *Cars* suggests that cars are important, taken for granted and human. Children can build up a dark and dangerous inner city environment and its antithesis, a green, peaceful suburb, using Lego. *Lego City* consists of derelict houses, police cars and criminals while *Lego Friends* is all about detached houses, flowers, children and playgrounds. As the children grow older they can become successful urban developers and build suburbs with private homes, high-rises and motorways in *Sim City*.

But everything is not green and shiny in American suburbia. Films like *Revolutionary Road, The Stepford Wives, Truman Show* and *Fun with Dick and Jane* suggest that life can also be lonely and anxiety-ridden. "This is my right; it is the right of every human being. I choose not the suffocating anaesthetic of the suburbs, but the violent jolt of the Capital. That is my choice," says Virginia Woolf, played by Nicole Kidman, in the film *The Hours*.

We are beginning to see other representations of city centres on the small screen. What do titles such as *Seinfeld, Friends, Sex and the City, How I Met Your Mother* and *Mad Men* evoke? They are all about busy city life characterised by a constant flow of social encounters and networking – but there are no children. This is all about young adults who are looking for partners and jobs, reinforcing the image of the city as unsuitable for families. If there are any children at all in shows that are set in the city, a much darker story is usually being told, as in *Chicago Hope, E.R.* or *The Wire*.

The stories and the images are clear and sharp. They represent the kind of cities we have been living in for the past fifty years. Cities we have designed and built; cities in which the distance between people is constantly increasing – "First we shape the city, then it shapes us."

Planners shaped the city

Five hundred senior traffic directors and politicians are laughing nervously. What on earth is the woman saying? That cities built for cars was a French idea? The former commissioner of the New York City Department of Transportation, Janette Sadik-Khan, is halfway through her keynote speech at the Designing Cities conference in San Francisco in 2014 when she drops the bomb.

"Americans actually think that walking and biking is a European thing, and that it doesn't fit in American cities, but guess where the idea of the car-oriented street came from? ..."[5] Sadik-Khan shows a picture of the Swiss-French architect Le Corbusier's *Plan Voisin for Paris* from 1925, a city cut through by highways and full of high-rises – a project sponsored by the French automobile manufacturer Voisin. Le Corbusier was a prominent modernist who in the 1920s and '30s contributed to a sea change in the approach to urban and community planning. The modernists wanted to do away with city streets and apartment blocks in order to get rid of the crowded, polluted environments that were the result of the 19th century industrialist boom. They dreamt of a city made up of parks and roads with freestanding tower blocks – cities made for cars and "modern man".[6] "The functional city" was to be divided up into areas of housing, areas for work and commercial centres.[7] Le Corbusier called his city of the future La Ville Radieuse.[8][9] And there were others; the American architect Frank Lloyd Wright's Broadacre City[10] from 1932 and the English architect Ebenezer Howard's Garden City[11] from 1902 are other utopian visions of green, sprawling suburban landscapes.[12] Janette Sadik-Khan wanted to convey to the audience in San Francisco that visions of the future do not always turn out the way people hope they will. "The automobile invasion of cities didn't just happen. It happened by design," she said. But you cannot blame the way cars have invaded our cities on car owners, the responsibility lies with politicians and urban planners.

Wide-spread motorism would of course not have been possible without the rapid development of the automotive industry in the early 1900s. It was when the assembly line production of cars took off that residential, small housing suburbs began to develop throughout the Western world. "The modern city is probably the most unlovely and artificial site this planet affords. The ultimate solution is to abandon it [...] We shall solve the City Problem by leaving the city," Henry Ford allegedly claimed in 1912. The automotive industry enjoyed massive support from the advertising industry, especially from Edward Bernays, the founder of public relations and brother of Sigmund Freud. Bernays promoted the automotive industry in general, and General Motors (GM) in particular, by describing cars not as a necessity, but as something to yearn for, a thing that spoke to your innermost desires. Car salesmen learned not to address the customers' intellect, which tells them what they need, but their emotions, which tell them that they will be a lot happier when they own a car. Influenced by Freud, Bernays gave the automotive industry the idea that cars are symbols of male sexuality. Bernays's collaboration with GM culminated in the Futurama exhibition at the New York World Exhibition in 1939 where a model of an ideal city, Democracity – City of the Future, was shown. It was an urban landscape with high-rise buildings and suburban sprawl designed around the car, an urban landscape that became very much a reality in the 20th century.

The new motorways and railway systems that were later purchased and subsequently phased-out by the automotive industry[13] allowed people to live outside the unhealthy city centres with their dirty workshops and factories. These city centres became even more unpleasant and harmful with the traffic that moved in from these very suburbs. Two hundred thousand people died in road accidents in the 1920s in the United States, and in 1925 alone, seven thousand children were killed as a result of being hit by a car.[14] On photographs from around the turn of the last century you can see how children played in the streets. The streets were dirty and the crowded flats disease-ridden, but it was still easier to move around than it is today.

In the 1940s, people were beginning to protest and organise local manifestations against the growing traffic. The journalist Jane Jacobs was among the more famous activists who fought for their own city district, Manhattan's Greenwich Village. Jacob's main adversary was Robert Moses, a man who exerted a major influence when it came to building freeways across New York City. Jacobs later wrote the classic *The Death and Life of Great American Cities,* a book about the street as a place for people of all ages and how this environment was being destroyed by developers, more specifically by the most prominent modernists represented by Le Corbusier and the International Congress of Modern Architecture (Congrès international d'architecture moderne, CIAM).

Le Corbusier allegedly said that, "The street wears us out. It is altogether disgusting. Why, then, does it still exist?" This is in direct opposition to Jacobs, who celebrated the street as the city's central nervous system and an important place for people to meet. Jacobs was also critical of the idea of the garden city, "a more harmonious combination of city and country, dwelling house and garden," as it was described in Raymond Unwin's manifesto *Nothing Gained by Overcrowding* (1912). The garden city was not representative of the density, diversity and dynamic that was the city's purpose according to Jacobs.

We now know that the modernists and the garden city proponents won and that they built the cities of North America and Europe after the war. These cities made for cars consisted mainly of suburban sprawl,[15] either in the form of large areas of small housing or groups of multi-storey buildings, office compounds and local commercial centres. Many residential areas are today heavily dependent on cars, but also those who live

The Americans' marriage with the car is more like an arranged marriage

in multi-storey housing or housing programmes travel by car to a higher degree. Even in suburbs served by metro or light railways, people are increasingly travelling by car.[16] Everything is further away when you are in the periphery.

"The Americans' marriage with the car is more like an arranged marriage," says Janette Sadik-Khan.[17] In the 20th century, town planners made sure that new city districts were adapted for cars, and as car prices dropped and more people could afford them, society became car-dependent. There was a rapid increase in the number of cars around 1950, after which it accelerated up to the early 2000s. In the United States, the automotive industry wielded significant power, and as early as in the 1920s car manufacturers and the newly formed auto clubs engaged in lobbying work that led to higher speed limits and more space for cars in the cities. According to Roy Chaplin, head of the Hudson Motor Car Company, "The automobile supplies a feeling of escape from this suppression of the individual, that is why the American public has seized upon motor travel so rapidly and with such intensity."[18] The term "jaywalking" – which in America insinuated the traffic sense of a country bumpkin – was invented by the car lobby. Federal guidelines forcing pedestrians to use pavements and pedestrian crossings came in 1928. They were implemented in hundreds of cities across the United States, and crossing a street anywhere else than on a pedestrian crossing became a criminal offence.

In his dissertation *Bilsamhället* (car society), Per Lundin offers a description of how this development in Sweden was primarily driven by experts and technocrats. "The car society was so much more than a solution to the problem of motorism. Not only did it suggest comfort, material wealth and movability, but also democracy and freedom," he argues. "Motorism is not a pastime for the wealthy, but an inescapable fact of progress. Our entire lifestyle is becoming Americanised," said the architect Sven Tynelius in 1956 after a study tour of the United States.[19]

One major milestone in Sweden was the Bilstaden (car city) conference, which was held at the Royal Institute of Technology in 1956, possibly inspired by the American car lobby's vision of "Motordom". Sweden's foremost functionalist, the architect Uno Åhrén, drew a great deal of inspiration from Le Corbusier, and he did not beat about the bush.

> We must be prepared to acknowledge that owning a car is a positive factor of great importance to the way we live. We must therefore investigate whether this does not mean that we need to start looking at urban development in a new way. A good way of going about this is to study how to plan for a "motorists' city", a new type of city that is truly designed with cars in mind.

The same year, the influential Chalmers professor Sune Lindström wrote a manifesto entitled *Framtidens stad* (city of the future):

> Our communities are now built around the car. Some time in the future, they will be completely adapted as they grow out of the virgin soil. In appearance, they will be both densely populated countryside and sparsely populated city. There will be a shopping centre consisting of only one or a few buildings surrounded by extensive, open parking lots that are five times the size of the shopping centre itself. But since we will by then have learned that parking is one of the most important functions of a city, we will also have come to realise

that these parking lots must be maintained and made beautiful in the same way as streets, public spaces and parks are. These large parking spaces will therefore be planted with trees in regular, attractive patterns. Near the shopping centre there will be schools, community halls, cinemas and service centres with laundromats, radio and car repair shops, et cetera. Groups of residential housing can be glimpsed in the distance. They are connected by means of motorways that are the spine of the community.

It is interesting to see how Sune Lindström's dream of the motorway as the spine of the community came true. These cities built for cars became a reality.

These cities were not only built as a result of the architects' fantasies about the future, there was political pressure coming from scientific institutions and organisations such as the Royal Automobile Club and other automobile associations as well as organisations affiliated with the petroleum industry, business and industry, the engineering community, commerce as well as the construction and transport industries that together supported a road network white paper that was carried by parliament in 1959. This document, *Vägplan för Sverige* (a road plan for Sweden), financed an extensive expansion of the road network for a period of twenty years in order to adapt it to the "demands" of motorism.[20]

Experts, researchers and non-profit organisations also contributed to establishing guidelines, standards and legislation that were implemented by the National Board of Public Building, the National Board of Housing, Building and Planning and the National Road Administration. The building code of 1960 prescribed eleven parking spaces per thousand square meters of living space. When *Riktlinjer för bebyggelseplanering med hänsyn till bilplatsbehov* – the official guidelines for allocating parking spaces in developed areas – was published in 1968 the number had increased to seventy spaces; but there were reactions to the increase. The following was printed in the daily newspaper *Dagens Nyheter*.[21]

There is a guaranteed standard only for cars, this "parking need" [...]
This is simply a question of politics, of values. What comes first, the
comfort of bus and train passengers or the comfort of motorists?
What distances are most important, the distance children travel to
day-care centres and schools, or the motorist's journey from home to
parking space? Is society meant only for motorists or for everyone?

The urban planners' bible in Sweden, *SCAFT 1968* (Stads-
byggnad, Chalmers, Arbetsgruppen för Trafiksäkerhet), described the layout of each city district in detail.[22]

SCAFT proscribed a separation of functions (home, work,
services) and of road users (cars and pedestrians).

The natural organisation of a car-dependent society consists of dense, car-free islands surrounded by roads and car parks. The car-free
islands may hold housing, shopping centres, offices, schools, etc.,

wrote Stig Nordqvist, a civil engineer.[23] Nordqvist exerted
a major influence on planning in Sweden in the 1950s and
'60s. His legacy is found in housing programmes such as Tensta
(Stockholm), Bergsjön (Gothenburg) and Vivalla (Örebro), all
characterized by a car-free central area surrounded by motorways. According to urban researchers Pia Björklid and Maria
Nordström, these principles are still valid and are much appreciated by the residents.[24] Footbridges and pedestrian underpasses allow children to easily reach schools and playgrounds,
but these housing programmes are still planned for cars. Similar city districts are today constructed in China and in the
Arabian Peninsula. These are designed specifically for car users.

Per Lundin notes that cars have become the norm throughout the Western hemisphere.[25]

Cars have been deliberately and successfully integrated into everyday life, and they are often indispensable in our professional as well
as our private lives [...] Cars have become part of the identity of
modern man [...] We are informed by this inner conflict. We have
become its prisoners whether we want it or not.

According to Lundin, criticism against a society based
around cars and the experts who voiced concern never enjoyed broad support among the population. Protest actions were

local and never had a national impact. Lundin concludes his dissertation by offering an account of what some of the most eager car advocates ended up doing later in life.

Olof Gunnarson, one of the SCAFT co-authors, later started the pedestrian organisation FOT. Later in life, the previously unyielding Stig Nordquist allegedly said that pedestrians should be the measure of the city. "Yes, we did make mistakes," admitted Sweden's equivalent of Le Corbusier, Uno Åhrén, and another SCAFT contributor, Sune Lindström, later asked himself, "How did it come to this?" Walter Gahn, co-author with, among others, Uno Åhrén of the modernist manifesto *Acceptera*, published in 1931, wrote in 1980,

> *Acceptera* came about in rather a hurry, and at a time when we were only at the beginning of these discussions, and almost nothing had been built yet [...] We probably under-estimated the psychological aspect, people's well-being and right to self-determination.[26]

Two years before he died in 1980, the father of the modern shopping mall, the American architect Victor Gruen, who had wanted to export city life to the suburbs, said that, "I refuse to pay alimony for those bastard developments. They ruined our cities."[27] The modernists wanted to do good, but many regretted it afterwards. They believed in change, progress and modern man, but they knew too little about how cities function. The large-scale experiments had large-scale effects. This is an uncomfortable and rather awkward fact. "All of the buildings, all of those cars/Were once just a dream/In somebody's head,"[28] sings Peter Gabriel ruefully in "Mercy Street".

The decision by experts, politicians and developers to place cars before people has turned out to have unexpected systemic effects. In the United States, three out of four people today use their car for journeys that are shorter than 1.5 kilometres.[29] In Europe, ninety per cent of all car travel is under six kilometres.[30] It is as if we have planned according to the principle, "it would be great if I could drive my car from A to B". If we add this principle, we eventually end up with an absurd society that will just make things worse for car owners. Hours spent in traffic jams and being obliged to drive your kids to school just because everybody else does. Planners sometimes say, "You are not stuck in traffic. You are traffic." Many of these systemic effects and the fact that more and more people are stuck in traffic can be blamed on urban sprawl. These cities create distance, not closeness.

Living with sprawl

In a report published by the London School of Economics I found some graphs that showed how people choose to travel in different cities, including Stockholm and Copenhagen.[31] It turned out that twenty per cent of the journeys made in Copenhagen were by bike compared to six per cent in Stockholm. This was no surprise. Anyone that has visited both cities will have noticed that people cycle more in Copenhagen than they do in Stockholm. What comes as a surprise is the number of car journeys – twenty-nine per cent for Stockholm and forty for Copenhagen. The London School of Economics is a highly reliable institution, so this information can hardly be wrong. I posted the figures on Twitter, asking why Copenhagen is so often set as an example when it turns out that people there drive more they do in, for example, Stockholm.

People were really upset by this, especially the cycling advocates on Twitter. I received a particularly strong comment from Mikael Colville-Andersen,[32] which made me realise that promoting bicycles is not necessarily the same thing as promoting less car traffic. The example of Copenhagen shows that you can encourage a lot of people to use their bikes if you have a good network of cycle lanes; maybe you could encourage even more people to abandon their cars if you have a well-functioning public transport system, as in Stockholm.

The obvious reason why people in Copenhagen drive more is that they do not have an extensive public transport system. Even though the Copenhagen city centre is larger than the Stockholm city centre, the suburbs there generate more

Variation in capacity and land use efficiency for different means of transport. A dedicated transit street is fifteen times more efficient than a street dedicated to private cars. (NACTO, Transit Street Design Guide, 2016)

Private motor vehicles
600 – 1600/HR

Mixed traffic with frequent buses
1000 – 2800/HR

Two way protected bikeway
7500/HR

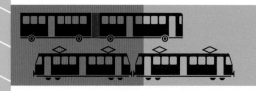

Dedicated transit lanes
4000 – 8000/HR

Pavement
9000/HR

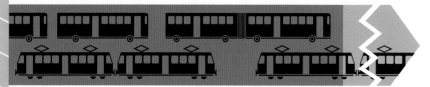

On-street transitway, bus or rail
10000 – 25000/HR

motorists. The dense city centre of Copenhagen with its excellent network of cycle lanes makes it a good example of a city for cyclists, while most Stockholm suburbs have excellent access to public transport. Perhaps car traffic in Stockholm would be reduced if the inferior cycle lanes system were upgraded. It would surely be a less expensive proposition than extending the public transport network in Copenhagen. Neither of these cities compare with super dense Hong Kong, where only seven per cent of the population travels by car and the average time people spend commuting is eleven minutes.[33]

Studies repeatedly show that there is a correlation between density and car use. The denser and more pedestrian- and cycle-friendly the city, the more people walk and cycle while fewer travel by car.[34] Not only does density generate ideal conditions for public transport, it also means that schools, day care centres, hospitals, commerce and jobs are located closer together, which makes it easy to cycle between them. Walking should not be underestimated as a means of transport. In Stockholm, thirty-four per cent of all travel is by foot while only twenty-nine per cent of the citizens travel by car.[40] In the dispersed city of Atlanta, ninety-two per cent travel by car.[41] It means that density is fundamentally important to social and economic development of a city. In Stockholm the average commute is thirty-four minutes. It corresponds to over six working weeks per year,[42] which means that Stockholmers spend more time commuting than on vacation. This is not evenly distributed. In the inner city district of Södermalm, thirteen per cent of residents own a car while the figure is forty-four per cent in the small housing suburb of Hässelby villastad. Few destinations are within walking distance there. According to a recent study, car use would fall by twenty to forty per cent if you double the density.[43] Another study shows that in comparison to more densely developed city districts, dispersed areas in the United States have sixty per cent higher car use and consume sixty to eighty per cent more land per capita.[44]

Let us take a closer look at the numbers. Stockholm city

34
min./day
=
6
weeks/year

34 min. commuting
equals 6 working
weeks in one year

"

If every citizen
lived in a de-
tached house
in 2050 these
would cover an
area the size of
India

"

now has a population of approximately 1.3 million people. In 2050, according to recent forecasts, approximately two million people will be living there.[45] If they were all house owners, the city would cover two thousand square kilometres and the distance from the city centre to the periphery would be fourteen kilometres, a distance that would take an hour to cover by bike. In this community of private housing there would be almost a million cars. If these two million people were to live in four to six storey buildings, the city centre would cover an area of 130 square kilometres, and the distance from the centre to the periphery would be 3.5 kilometres, which could be covered in fifteen minutes by bike. There would be about a quarter of a million cars, a quarter of the number of cars calculated for the urban sprawl scenario. Let us now look at the bigger picture. The urban population in the developing world is expected to increase by 2.2 billion by 2050. If these people were living in detached homes, it would require an area of 4.4 million square kilometres, an area larger than India. Were they to live in a dense city, the required area would fall to a tenth of that figure.[46] These calculations are hypothetical of course, the truth is likely to be somewhere in between, but it demonstrates why so many experts and politicians take urban sprawl seriously.

The density of the city affects citizens in several ways. Travel distances are shorter in dense cities, with fewer emissions as a result. This can be illustrated by comparing Atlanta and Barcelona, each with a population of five million. The city of Atlanta is almost eight thousand square kilometres and Barcelona is 650. Calculations show that in Atlanta, carbon emissions are seven tonnes a year per capita just for transport. In Barcelona the figure is just over a tonne, merely one fifth of Atlanta's emissions.[47]

There is extensive research on the correlation between the density of a city and its emissions. According to an American study, an expansion of suburban sprawl by ten per cent would increase carbon emissions by over five per cent per capita, and other emissions by almost ten per cent.[48] The UN Intergovernmental Panel on Climate Change's (IPCC) latest report says that, "Key urban form drivers of greenhouse gas emissions are density, land use mix, connectivity, and accessibility."[49] The extent of hard surfaces has a major effect on climate change, caus-ing increased surface water runoff, which may cause floo-ding as well as greater temperature fluctuations and greater heat output as a result. This is a serious problem when it comes to the health of small children and the elderly in cities with a warm climate.[50] According to one study, areas of dispersed small hous-ing require three times the amount of asphalt per capita as a densely populated city.[51]

Less density leads to increased traffic and emissions as well as a higher number of road accidents according to the World Resources Institute. The number of road accidents in dispersed cities is between two and five times that of denser cities.[52] In the dispersed city of Atlanta, for example, ten in a hundred thousand people die as a result of road accidents while the much more dens-ely populated New York City has three road deaths per hundred thousand citizens.[53] Yet another study reports that an increase in population density by forty people per square kilometre redu-ces the number of road accidents by six per cent.[54] These results compare well with data that shows that the more time people spend driving their cars on average in an American state, the greater the number of road deaths per capita in that state.[55]

According to the United Nations Human Settlements Pro-gramme, UN Habitat, a sustainable urban density is reached at 150 people per 0.01 km^2 (roughly corresponding to one neigh-bourhood block of buildings that are four storeys or higher).[56] In their definition of sustainable density, this degree of density provides the best basis for collective and cost-effective solutions in terms of transport, water, sanitation and other infrastructure. Recent research shows that urban sprawl is not financially viab-le, it probably costs the United States over a thousand billion dollars a year.[57] Forty per cent of this vast sum is external ex-penditure, what society has to pay for road construction and maintenance, emissions, congestion, healthcare, et cetera. Sixty

"sustainable density" =

150+

persons per hectare

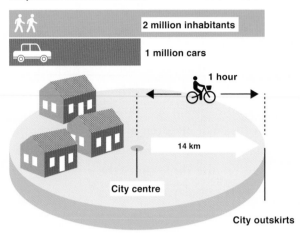

Dispersed Stockholm 2050

2 million inhabitants

1 million cars

1 hour

14 km

City centre

City outskirts

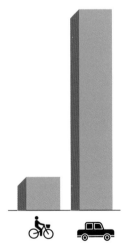

Cost to society

The cost to society is six times higher when you travel by car than by bike

per cent is attributed to internal expenditure, that is to say the cost to each individual for travel time, loss of income, keeping a car, health issues, et cetera.

The Canadian think-tank Sustainable Prosperity has estimated the cost for law enforcement, healthcare, fire services, roads, parks, water and sewage to be twice as high in a dispersed suburban community. One household in a densely populated city costs 1,500 dollars a year while a household in a small housing community costs society 3,400 dollars a year.[58] According to an American study, a fire station in a suburb with many cul-de-sacs costs four times as much to maintain as a fire station in a densely populated city.[59] These costs also affect each individual citizen and their chances to achieve economic mobility. On average, if City A is twice as dense as City B, children from low-income families in City A will be 41 per cent more likely to reach the top five per cent of income earners than children from low-income families in City B. The economist and Nobel laureate Paul Krugman writes that,[60]

> [Sprawl] would make an effective public transportation system nearly impossible to operate even if politicians were willing to pay for it, which they aren't. As a result, disadvantaged workers often

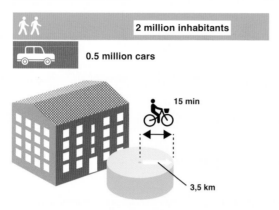

Dense Stockholm 2050

2 million inhabitants

0.5 million cars

15 min

3,5 km

find themselves stranded; there may be jobs available somewhere, but they literally can't get there.

The cost of one journey depends on the means of transportation. Calculations distinguish between the cost for the individual – travel time, accident risk, vehicle repairs and public transport fares – and costs to society – construction and infrastructure maintenance, health effects and environmental impact. If your journey costs one dollar, the cost to society is one cent if you walk and eight cents if you travel by car.[61] According to a recent study of Copenhagen, the cost to society is six times higher when you travel by car than when you travel by bike.[62] The difference is so great that not even a miscalculation changes the conclusion that car traffic is heavily subsidised, and that a denser city is both more economically viable and environmentally sustainable.

"People who walk, bike and take public transit are effectively subsidizing the least efficient transportation mode at the expense of their own way of getting around," says Janette Sadik-Khan,[63] and according to the London School of Economics, "More compact urban growth, aligned with the increased provision of public transport infrastructure and services and pro-active support for non-motorised transport use, is likely to deliver substantial net economic and social benefits."[64]

"I would have been dead if I had lived in a town," reads the headline of an article published in the magazine *Skärgården.*[65] An elderly man who suffered a heart attack in his home on an island in the Stockholm archipelago recounts how quickly a helicopter had picked him up, and that an ambulance in town would have cost him his life if it had become stuck in traffic. Naturally, anyone living and working outside the city has a right to health care and service, but in a world of diminishing resources and climate change, helicopter transport is a somewhat problematic issue. In the Brazilian mega city of São Paulo, wealthy people have started to travel by helicopter between the skyscrapers due to the traffic situation on the ground.[66] A city that solves its traffic problems by resorting to helicopters will be looking at some hard economic and ecological issues in the future. A friend of mine was closer to a more realistic scenario. He told me about having suffered a heart attack, about the ride in an ambulance to hospital and the competent hospital team that received him. "If I hadn't lived in a city I would probably have been dead now," he said.

Finding exact definitions of sprawl and density is not that simple. There are many ways of measuring density. The Norwegian urban researcher Peter Næss has shown that distance to the city centre can explain why people travel by car just as adequately as population density. The point he makes is that cities are fundamentally monocentric, and that it does not matter all that much if a dense city district is located in the city periphery; people will still need to use their cars.[67] Næss' conclusions compare well with traffic researcher Daniel Jonsson's studies that show how car use in the periphery is greater than in the centre despite access to a metro system.[68] Against this background it is clear that constructing more densely populated cities does not suffice as a measure for reducing car use. A key factor is to develop areas that are as close as possible to the city centre. It is very much the reason why densification is now being discussed, not only in Swedish cities;

scholars and planners across the world are currently studying and discussing the form and structure of dense cities.

The demographer Wendel Cox, who wrote the book *War on the Dream: How Anti-Sprawl Policy Threatens the Quality of Life*,[69] and the urban researcher Joel Kotkin are highly critical towards urbanists such as Edward Glaeser and Richard Florida. Cox is now using families as a weapon in the debate. In his article "The Childless City", Kotkin wrote, "What is a city for? Ever since cities first emerged thousands of years ago, they have been places where families could congregate and flourish."[70] In another article he says that,

> Perhaps most important, dense places tend to be regarded as poor places for raising families. In simple terms, a dense future is likely to be a largely childless one [...] All for a [density] policy that, for all its progressive allure, will make more Americans more unhappy, less familial, and likely poorer.[71]

When I speak to parents, they find it normal to "move out", that is to say to the suburbs, "for the children's sake". This has been the case for the past fifty years. Even the super-urbanist Edward Glaeser, who wrote a much-debated book entitled The Triumph of the City, and who grew up on Manhattan, says that he was compelled to move to a house in the suburbs when his children were born.[72]

Why do young families want to live in the suburbs? Apart from owning a garden, "where the children can play", in a contained, safe neighbourhood, Joel Kotkin stresses a safe street environment, parks, more living space and the quality of schools. This is a typical illustration of the North American point of view. These are qualities that are just as possible to achieve in a dense city too, and they do exist to various degrees in European city centres where children are more visible than in the United States. Fifty thousand children live within the boundaries of central Stockholm; the same number as in the whole of Uppsala, Sweden's fourth city. Much to everyone's surprise, the Hammarby Sjöstad development became one of the most child-rich neighbourhoods in Stockholm. I asked Glaeser if he believes it is possible to limit the demand for sparsely populated suburbia, and he replied that he believes it is, but that nothing will change until inner cities are able to offer better schools, which is in fact the case in Europe, especially in Scandinavia.[73] Northern European cities are also better suited for children, partly because they are pedestrian-friendly. "My son and I have moved in to town, and I have just realised that the best way of getting about is by foot," says Permanent Secretary Sara Danius of the Swedish Academy in an interview.[74]

So it appears that density can be either good or bad. While I was working on my PhD I explored the correlation between density and green space. Two mutually independent surveys were conducted in the city of Stockholm. They showed no correlation between density and the way people experienced access to parks and nature.[75] [76] Instead, they revealed that in some areas of the densely populated inner city centre people are less concerned with lack of vegetation than in some much more dispersed suburbs. It was perplexing. Why do we have such different views on vegetation? I began to play around with different measures of green open spaces and density in an attempt to solve this conundrum. After extensive research I found an answer that statistically could explain the discrepancy. The four determining factors were the size and quality of green spaces (their utility value), how close they were and how easy they were to navigate in. Density had nothing to do with it; instead, experience of green areas was almost entirely dependent on their design and location.[77] Most of the parks in Stockholm are, in fact, found in the city centre.

This means that it is possible to construct a city that has both density and vegetation, because everything seems to depend on how parks are designed and located. If this offers city dwellers proximity and quality of life, density matters less. It is even necessary for maintaining various qualities in green open spaces. Like any other type of service, playgrounds, sports grounds, lawns and other meeting places require the presence of people. A park with no people is a pretty useless park, as

Jane Jacobs points out.[78] Is it possible to increase development density in an area while at the same time adding more green open spaces? The answer is yes! Many suburbs are separated by roads, green spaces have low utility and in some cases are hardly used at all. As density increases, it is possible to build better footpaths to existing green areas where utilities such as playgrounds, sports grounds, footpaths, picnic areas, sun bathing, bbq areas, allotments and ecosystem services can be added. Well-functioning, large parks are crucial when it comes to preventing urban sprawl.

So what is the correlation between density and congestion? Would a larger, denser city automatically cause greater congestion? Not necessarily. First of all, people travel less by car in dense city environments. The number of car journeys can be up to ten times larger in dispersed, peripheral suburbs than in the city centre.[79] The fact is that the existing road and street network can cope with more cars. Urban researcher Anders Gullberg has shown how the existing infrastructure could be put to better use.[80] There are, on average, four empty seats in every car. Queues only occur on short stretches and over limited periods. Small reductions in the number of cars at those points will increase capacity since queuing can reduce the flow to almost zero. Self-driving vehicles that are able to communicate with each other can choose other routes and increase capacity many times over in the grid as a whole. Buses that run in bus lanes can accommodate fifteen times as many passengers as cars. Metros and trams have a capacity sixty times greater than that of cars. According to Anders Gullberg, it is smarter to exploit the existing infrastructure before you start to build new roads, not least because new roads as a rule generate even more traffic. "Adding motorway lanes to deal with traffic congestion is like loosening your belt to cure obesity,"[81] is a statement attributed to the urban researcher Lewis Mumford. "You can't build your way out of congestion,"[82] is the short and simple advice that many traffic planners serve up today.

The twenty-first century opened with a wave of urbanisation.

Statistics show that we may have reached "peak car", and the increasing use of cars is being debated.[83] According to the experts, there are specific reasons why people drive less in city centres these days.[84] People are more interested in quality time – with the demise of the nuclear family and the housewife, driving a car and spending time in transit are seen as a waste of time – when both parents work, living near the city centre is a more gender equal solution; People tend to prioritize spending time with their family over playing space for their children as they try to put together the pieces of the life puzzle; An aging population requires proximity to services and healthcare; City centres are becoming denser in terms of housing and workplaces, and public transport systems are built out on a global scale; The use of smartphones and social media demands meeting places and urban environments. As we are approaching peak oil we may also expect increasing oil prices, so there is no longer a correlation between economic growth and motoring.[85] The noisy, dirty factories that once gave rise to suburbia and modernism have moved out of the city centres. Today, pollution is instead caused by car traffic.

The Swiss-French architect Le Corbusier allegedly said that we must "kill the street". Le Corbusier is the godfather of modernist urban development. In the 1920s and '30s he wrote a string of books on the changing city, and he co-founded the Congrès international d'architecture moderne (CIAM), which subsequently published a manifesto (*Charte d'Athenes*) that came to inform urban planning from the 1920s onwards. In 1933, Le Corbusier proposed that the entire Stockholm city centre should be demolished and replaced with a few large, meandering buildings.[86] He has recently been severely criticized for his Fascist and Nazi connections, his contacts with totalitarian regimes and for his elitist ideology of segregation, which I will not elaborate on here.[87] The modernist vision and its urban development programme had a massive impact on urbanism in the 20th century when city districts and a completely new type of city came to the fore. Few people were able to predict the consequences. It was a gigantic social experiment that did not always turn out the way the architects envisaged. But the street is not dead; in 1981 the American architect Donald Appleyard wrote that,

> People have always lived on streets. They have been the places where children first learned about the world, where neighbors met, the social centers of towns and cities, the rallying points for revolts, the scenes of repression [...] The street has always been the scene of this conflict, between living and access, between resident and traveler, between street life and the threat of death.[89]

The street is in fact alive and well; street space and closeness have become key issues in contemporary urbanism practice.

Who gets city space

In one of his public talks, the Mayor of Bogotá, Enrique Peñalosa, asks his audience, "In what country is parking a constitutional right?"[90] Peñalosa is renowned for his urban reforms. Like Robin Hood, he took money from major motorway developments and used it for building schools, libraries, and bus and cycle routes in deprived areas of the city. Peñalosa has visited Sweden several times. Sweden's largest construction company invited him to what turned out to be the most visited seminar during the country's most important forum for Swedish politics, the Almedalen Week, in 2013. He was impressed by the way politicians were able to take over the Visby city centre and that the meetings took place in a car-free city environment. Peñalosa also spoke at an architectural event in Stockholm the same year, and I had the pleasure of guiding him around Stockholm. We walked through the wealthy central district of Östermalm before we took the metro to Husby, one of Stockholm's most deprived suburbs.

On Sturegatan Peñalosa started, grabbed me by the arm and asked me who, "gave these people the right to store their private stuff here [...] in public space?" Although I have been living in the city all of my life, I have never really thought about parking spaces in that way. Travelling by car benefits the person who drives the car. Everyone else must give way, wait, and move aside. Naturally, I sometimes travel by taxi or rental car, but it benefits no one but me. When I do, I am the one that threatens and invades other people's space in the city. I do benefit from goods transports, but not from private car traffic. Pedestrians and cyclists gain little from drivers. All of a sudden I began to view the street differently. Who is it for? Who benefits, and who misses out?

Peñalosa received death threats after he had removed all the parking spaces from central Bogotá. People who were living and trading along the streets were wondering where to park their cars. Peñalosa just told them that they were responsible for their own private property. The city takes no responsibility for how you store either your clothes or your cars. As so often when parking spaces are removed, real estate prices soared as did the turnover for the shops along the street.[91]

Peñalosa was also deeply committed to bus users' right to use the street. "A bus with a hundred people has a right to hundred times more road space than a car with one." It is not only a question of rights, but of efficiency. Anyone can understand, said Peñalosa, that if more people travel by bus the traffic flows better and you spend less money on road construction and maintenance. Transport for New South Wales in Sydney have calculated that the people in one subway train take as much space as fifteen buses or up to a thousand cars. A bus lane has up to fifteen times greater capacity for transporting people than a car lane, which means that one bus lane would have to be replaced with fifteen car lanes to be as efficient.[92] If you removed all public transport on Manhattan, you would need forty-eight eight-lane car bridges to allow the same number of people to travel to and from the island.[93]

There are currently about one billion cars in the world. In 2030 the number is estimated to be two billion and in 2050 three billion according to International Energy Agency forecasts.[94] The surface requirements alone generated by these three billion cars (about ten square metres per car) corresponds to the surface of Belgium, which is thirty thousand square kilometres. The

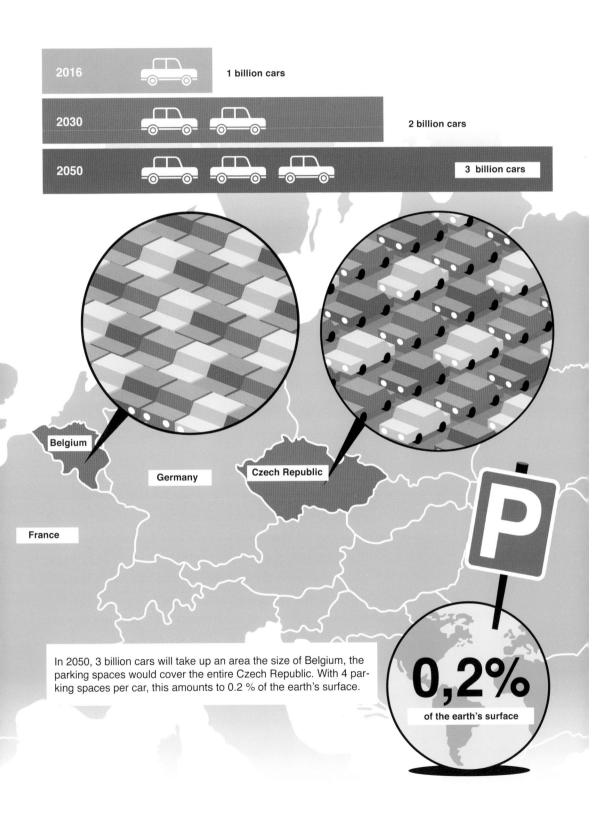

2016 — 1 billion cars

2030 — 2 billion cars

2050 — 3 billion cars

Belgium

Germany

Czech Republic

France

P

0,2%
of the earth's surface

In 2050, 3 billion cars will take up an area the size of Belgium, the parking spaces would cover the entire Czech Republic. With 4 parking spaces per car, this amounts to 0.2 % of the earth's surface.

**There is an
estimated half a
billion parking
spaces in the
United States as
a whole**

surface area needed for parking (about twenty-five square metres per car) corresponds to the surface of the Czech Republic. A normal estimate is approximately three to five parking spaces per car, so just the parking spaces needed for all the cars that will exist in 2050 would take up 0.2 per cent of the earth's surface. Add to that all the roads and streets these additional two million cars require. There are about five and a half million cars in Sweden today. Car ownership is around four hundred in a thousand citizens, or forty per cent.[95] It means that just under half of Sweden's population are car owners. The problem of the amount of space needed for cars is most urgent in our cities where space is scarce. Twenty per cent of a Swedish city centre is normally dedicated to traffic; twenty per cent is parking spaces. In the County of Stockholm the total parking area may today be up to sixteen square kilometres, which corresponds to approximately half of the city centre. There are approximately nineteen million parking spaces in Los Angeles[96] – fourteen per cent of the entire city.[97] There is an estimated half a billion parking spaces in the United States as a whole.[98] Knowing that one single car requires more space on average than one person's living space it is hard to argue that a city built to accommodate cars is very efficient in terms of space.[99] Add to that the fact that a motorist occupies a time space (the space one person uses during a certain time period in a certain vehicle) that is a thousand times that of a person who travels by public transport.[100] Compare that to the fact that you can fit ten bikes into a regular parking space.

Land is scarce in dense cities. Nevertheless, parking fees are only levied on some public land. Even in very attractive locations, the municipality usually offers residents parking permits at a very low cost. If the same property were instead rented out at a market price, the revenue would be many times higher. The sixty largest densely populated municipalities in Sweden miss out on about 1.8 billion dollars. Parking spaces along the streets of these municipalities correspond to 150 square kilometres of developable land area to a value of approximately

37 billion dollars and a development potential corresponding to one and a half million new flats. In the form of tenant-owner flats in Stockholm these would cost approximately eleven billion dollars. Conversely, it means that if tenant-owner flats were as generously priced as residents' permits, you would be able to buy a sixty-square-metre flat for under 25,000 dollars.[101] In the book *Trafikmaktordningen* the organisation Planka.nu reveals that parking fines are between 60 and 112 dollars, while travelling on public transport without a valid ticket would set you back 150 dollars.[102]

What about the expenditure and revenue associated with parking on privately developed land? A space in a local residents' car park normally costs around sixty thousand dollars to construct. Despite the high production cost, a normal tariff for a parking space in a garage in a suburb near Stockholm is only one hundred dollars a month, which means that someone other than the person who is using the parking space is bearing most of the cost. If you live in a relatively new development and do not own a car, you are paying between 125 and 375 dollars more for your home each month so the person who does have a car does not have to pay the full amount. When you buy that flat you are in effect enabling others to afford a car, ultimately putting more cars on the roads.

The number of cyclists is exploding. In Stockholm, it has trebled in the past twenty years and in New York it has doubled over a period of five years. More cyclists require more space, and for good reasons. A bicycle only needs a sixth of the space of a car, it produces no emissions, it is petroleum-free and the beneficial health effects are many. Bikes can replace both short and long car journeys. The average cycle commuter in Stockholm travels ten kilometres by bike and is thereby able to cover a large part of the city. The fact is that cycling is the fastest way to get from door to door in a reasonably dense urban environment. About half the cyclists in Copenhagen claim that they cycle because it is the quickest way to get around.[103] This increase in cycling depends on a number of factors. Right now, there

Stockholm

🚲　　🚲🚲🚲

⊢———— 20 years ———→

New York

🚲　　🚲🚲

⊢———— 5 years ———→

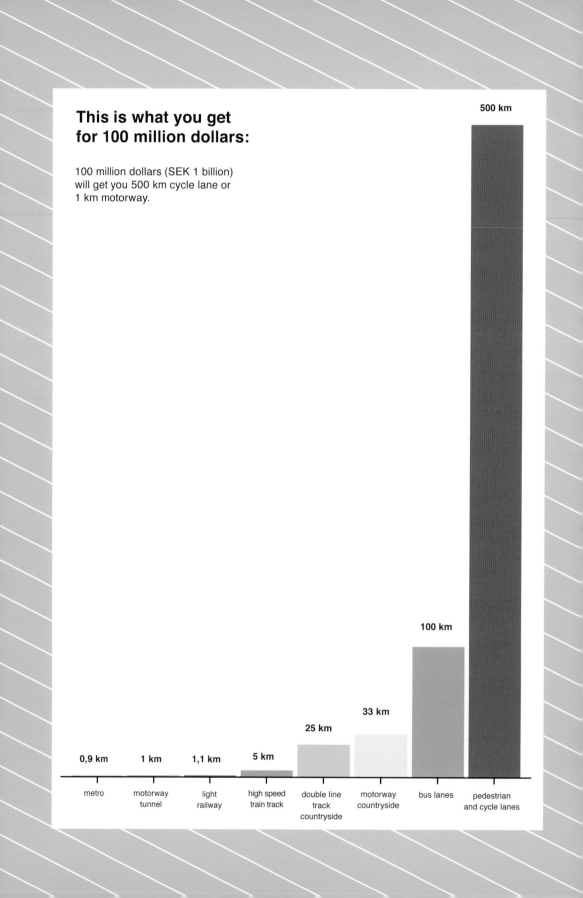

are two main reasons. One is that municipalities are making it easier for cyclists to get around, another is the fact that the urban life style has become trendy, and if you cycle to work it means that you are living in a central, urban environment.

More cyclists and fewer motorists mean a cleaner, less noisy city. While this is true, we should not forget that bikes are vehicles too. They are "softer" than cars, but a bicycle is still a vehicle that can easily reach speeds of up to forty kilometres per hour. That is not the kind of missile you can negotiate with. It has the capacity to kill a pedestrian, which is rare, but it does occur. Developers have a bad habit of combining pedestrians and cyclists as if they were one and the same and are prone to building combined cycle and pedestrian zones. It may look good on paper, but in reality it causes conflicts and people living in dense urban environments are finding it more and more irritating. Especially in places where lycra-clad commuters race in to town from suburban separated cycle zones and hit the city streets at high speed.

These cyclists often demand "cycle highways", wide cycle lanes free of intersections and pedestrians. Speed and navigability are paramount in their view. One much discussed cycle highway, the so-called *cykelslangen* (the cycle snake), was recently completed between Vesterbro and Islands brygge in Copenhagen. It is a raised, meandering flyover that runs like a speed track through the harbour. Many cyclists love it, because it connects the long commuter zones, rather like motorways do for cars. A similar idea, Skycycle, has been proposed for London, but these cycle superhighways do not encourage urban life. You cannot simply stop to have a chat or do a bit of shopping; they are just as focused on speed as motorways are. The rather puzzling term "cycle superhighways" is common in discussions about building fast cycle lanes. The rhetoric is beginning to sound more like that which is associated with cars. We are becoming a society of cyclists. "Plan for bikes – think in terms of cars!" was a recent tweet from one influential developer of cycle lanes, Krister Isaksson. In the book *Roads Were Not*

Built for Cars: How Cyclists Were the First to Push for Good Roads and Became the Pioneers of Motoring[104] you can read about how cyclists pioneered road construction and that the automotive industry at the end of the 19th century was very much dependent on the bicycle industry. Even the father of mass motoring, Henry Ford, seems to have been a keen cyclist.

The Danish PR organisation Cycling Embassy of Denmark[105] promotes Copenhagen as the best city in the world for cyclists with the help of urban design stars such as Jan Gehl and Mikael Colville-Andersen. They like to talk about cycling as a kind of faster way of walking – a pleasant social activity. But when you cycle in Copenhagen or Amsterdam you get a sense of the high pace and a rather advanced cycling culture. People shout and ring their bells if others fail to follow the rules. What would happen if pedestrians were to do the same, ring a bell as soon as someone got in their way or walked too slowly; they don't fortunately, because they are not vehicles. Cyclists, like motorists, are keen to protect their rights. Cyclists demand more space in the city, which is fine if that space is taken away from cars, the trouble is that it happens at the expense of pedestrians. It has become all too common for municipalities to use half the pavement for cycle lanes instead of building them across parking spaces or sections of road. The fact that the City of New York has built 560 kilometres of new cycle lanes over the past few years is commendable, but it has also caused a great deal of conflict between motorists and pedestrians. Several law firms in New York now specialize in cycling accidents.

Developers are now recommending protected bike lanes.[106] These are placed between the pavement and the street parking. It has turned out to be a very safe solution. The parked cars protect the cyclists from road traffic. There are fewer cycle accidents, cyclists feel safer, and as a result more people feel more confident using their bikes. To get a large number of people to cycle requires, more than anything, a safe and secure cycling environment throughout the city.[107] Strong, intrepid risk-takers (men) are already cycling. The development of new cycle zones should benefit those who feel less safe. Continued construction of protected cycle lanes is an important tool to this end. Oslo[108] and Stockholm[109] have chosen different strategies where Stockholm has almost exclusively focused on fast lanes, but who is most vulnerable? How are pedestrians protected? On the main Stockholm thoroughfares, cyclists race past pedestrians and children on pavements at thirty kilometres an hour. Both motorists and cyclists are driving, or riding, a vehicle and both demand their own space, which can endanger pedestrians, especially those who have trouble dealing with fast-moving traffic such as children, the elderly and the disabled.

One striking example is a section of the lower part of Götgatan in Stockholm. It was converted into a pedestrian precinct in 2004. Cyclists are allowed there because Götgatan is the busiest road in Stockholm and also a shortcut through town.[110] Most cyclists travelling from the south towards the city centre pass through this stretch of street. The pedestrian precinct has also become a busy area with buskers and shoppers. Cycle commuters and city planners are not too happy, however. "This is a warning example [...] It's classified as a priority cycle zone. It's weird the way they have combined pedestrians and cyclists since we have very different road behaviour," says one cyclist.[111]

The question is whether anyone has greater priority in the streetspace. Is the city a place for people to meet and interact, or is it made for traffic? Most modern cities – Stockholm, Vancouver and New York, for example – prioritize pedestrians, then come cyclists, public transport, goods transport, taxis and private cars in that order. In the same way as cars should give way to buses, cycles should give way to pedestrians. Many pedestrians do not feel safe walking on the cycle/pedestrian section of Götgatan; this is not the way forward for a city that wants become more attractive. Bikes are essential in a city where there are fewer cars, but like car traffic, cycle traffic must not be developed at the pedestrians' expense. They are at the very heart of city life. When it comes down to it, we are all pedestrians. It is what makes us all equal.

In 2012, the City of Stockholm commissioned a major survey of central Stockholm.[112] I was involved in analysing housing, offices, commerce, the environment, the streetscape and traffic flows. We calculated pedestrian flows, cycle flows and traffic flows; we measured street width, pavement width and traffic lane width. We then divided the number of pedestrians and motorists with the width of the pavement and the road respectively, which showed that motorists were allowed five times the space of pedestrians on Klarabergsgatan, 3.8 on Vasagatan, 2.8 on south Götgatan, 2.6 on Regeringsgatan, 2.4 on Kungsgatan, 2.1 on St. Eriksgatan and so on.[113] It is remarkable that a city, which in the structure plan is described as a "pedestrian city" with an "accessibility strategy" that puts pedestrians first and cars last. Allocating twice as much space for motorists as for pedestrians makes no sense.

What will happen now to those of us crowding together on the edge of the pavement? How are we to cross the road? We usually have to wait for a green light at a pedestrian crossing. The traffic lights are rarely discussed when we talk about the right to city space. It is an invisible problem because it is ultimately a question of how the engineers program them. According to the city traffic administration there are no political directives for how motorists and pedestrians are to share the street space and how long one is supposed to wait for the other.[114] The engineers are focused on reducing congestion, so in the service of encouraging an even flow, they allocate more space to cars. As a pedestrian in Stockholm I can easily verify that this is true. I have made some highly unscientific measurement on waiting times at some major traffic points in central Stockholm. The most common ratio is one to six. Where cars are allowed about sixty seconds to pass an intersection, pedestrians get ten seconds to cross the road. This applies to the larger thoroughfares in central Stockholm where the flow of cars and pedestrians is even. It is like a supermarket with six tills for men and only one for women. It would matter less if car traffic actually contributed to every city dweller's quality of life, but what is happening now is that precedence is given to something that is intrusive and that can cause injury and death; something that creates distance instead of closeness. How did this come about?

Motorism is our livelihood

I received an e-mail from a colleague who works with traffic planning in New York City.

> What is the latest on the Slussen redevelopment? I read here that the project was put on hold and I see that there is opposition. What do you see as the reasons for that? From what I see in these designs, there would be a lot more pedestrian and bike space, whereas now there is mostly space for roads. Who would you say is leading the opposition?[115]

The issue here is the much-debated Slussen project, a traffic solution that was implemented in central Stockholm in 1935, and which is now being demolished and redeveloped. At the time, architects and engineers believed that this was what the city of the future would look like; Le Corbusier even sent a note of encouragement.[116] Slussen was designed for cars, for traffic flows so great that they do not even exist today. There was strong belief in the future and in the future of cars as well as in the project's architectural design.

I replied to my American colleague that the project had been endorsed and that everything seemed to be going according to plan. How many that are in fact opposed to the project is not clear, but the opinions of several Stockholm celebrities were put forward in the media.

> Glad to hear it's going ahead. Always strange when people you would expect to be otherwise progressive on urban issues turn out to be fans of the status quo on the streets. We certainly saw plenty of that in New York as well.

He was referring to a redesign of the streets of New York in 2007–2013 under Mayor Michael Bloomberg when car spaces were removed, pavements were widened and new cycle lanes were built. The former commissioner of the New York Department of Transportation, Janette Sadik-Khan, has described the

Owning a car costs 600 dollars a month.

$ 600

For the same amount you could:

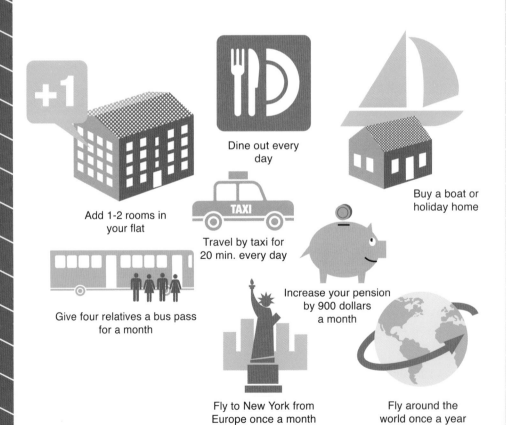

Add 1-2 rooms in your flat

Dine out every day

Buy a boat or holiday home

Travel by taxi for 20 min. every day

Give four relatives a bus pass for a month

Increase your pension by 900 dollars a month

Fly to New York from Europe once a month

Fly around the world once a year

struggle to achieve this in her book *Streetfight – Handbook for an Urban Revolution.*[117] Much of the book is about how hard it is to break the status quo, not least when it comes to getting rid of cars and parking spaces in order to make way for bikes and pedestrians. When Sadik-Khan spoke at the Citymoves conference in Stockholm, she also mentioned the Slussen project. "It takes guts [for politicians] to overcome a loud opposition, nostalgic of a place that only a Volvo would love," she said.

I have had the pleasure of working on the Slussen Project for the City of Stockholm. Alongside the external media debate, I have been able to follow internal discussions between architects, engineers and economists. I was between 2009 and 2012 responsible for pedestrian accessibility and public spaces for the urbanism consultancy Spacescape, and we studied the existing Slussen installation very closely. We looked at pedestrian flows, how the area was used and its contribution to the cityscape,[118] and there were numerous issues. Slussen is the most complex location Spacescape have ever been involved in. How much space should be allocated for pedestrians? How wide should the pavements be? Where should steps be placed? Are overpasses necessary? Should there be a park? How big should it be? Where will the cars be driving? Where will they not be driving?

Each meeting involved a struggle, a fight for every inch. We lost many battles: the pedestrian bridge, the terminal, flights of steps, pavement widths, public squares, vistas. Some of our suggestions were included in the plan, such as the park, the terraces, the wide car-free quays, the situation of certain steps and pedestrian precincts. I am especially pleased about Katarinaparken, the park by the lift, and the terraces with a view of Stockholm. But I will never forget the fight over the pedestrian bridge between Munkbron in the Old Town and Södermalmstorg on the Slussen side. At one meeting the city architect told us it was too ugly and that it was superfluous because there were other ways of crossing the water. We believed we could prove the opposite through zone analyses and calculations of distances to services. However, after too many hard fights the

City decided to phase us out. We were quite simply becoming too difficult to handle. After 2012 we were no longer involved in the project or able to influence the design. Today, I feel rather ambivalent about this situation.

Completion of the Slussen development that is now underway is forecast for 2022. It is not the creation of a single celebrity architect, but the result of a complex web of decisions and solutions that have been negotiated under pressure from experts, architects, politicians and the general public. It seems that no one is entirely satisfied, myself included. But the question is how it will look and how it will perform when everything is in place. The truth is, no one knows – including us, the experts that have done our utmost to model and simulate this proposal. Yet so many people are absolutely firm in their beliefs, including most of the more famous Stockholm profiles;[119] well-reputed architects[120] have expressed their frustration, wishing that the Slussen of 1935 be preserved. I have no trouble understanding that. Old buildings and city locations are associated with a past that is always worth preserving. Also, many amazing cultural events have taken place here, clubs and concerts I have visited and loved. However much I try to look at it from every angle, the Slussen of 1935 – just as Sergels torg, built in 1957 – represents a dream a society that in the future would be dependent on cars, with cars travelling over ground and pedestrians in tunnels under ground. International visitors, including Janette Sadik Khan, Enrique Peñalosa, Charles Montgomery (Happy City) and Ethan Kent (Project for Public Spaces), all confirm this. Slussen is a fascinating and complex site, but it has not been created with a focus on pedestrians. It is a powerful symbol that every day and every hour of the day affirms the importance of motorism, like a cog in the car city machinery.

Building a city based on car transport is a constantly self-generating process where cars are allocated value, become necessary and generate traffic. As more and more people drive cars, the demand for using cars increases among those who do not yet drive. It is not only a question of status, but to own a car in order to cope with everyday life in a city where an increasing number of services can only be reached by car. The following can be found on the car lobby organisation Bil Sweden's web site.

Road transport is fundamental to the welfare of our elongated country. Cars offer a flexibility and freedom of choice in everyday life that few other means of transport can offer. Thanks to cars and roads, we can choose to live our lives far from the city in sparsely populated areas and still be able to drive our children to football training or horse riding, we can go shopping and we can travel to meet friends and family. People who live in an urban environment often also need a car to make everyday life work.[121]

Notice how they claim that you "choose" to live in a sparsely populated area and how the car then becomes "necessary" for making life work. This is precisely what motorism is all about, a deliberate free choice that subconsciously leads to dependence and lack of freedom. Many make a living out of this dependence.

Those who most benefit from a car-dependent society are those who already own a car. If you have invested in a car, you will of course want to know that everything you need can be reached by car, and the more people that drive, the more adapted to cars society becomes – until you get stuck in a queue. Then all other cars are simply obstacles. People who are extremely dependent on their car often live outside town in places that are not served by public transport.[122] One of the reasons you make that choice is perhaps that you do not want to be disturbed by cars, but the more people that make this choice, the more traffic you get, which means that more and more people move even further away from the city centres. Those who do not own a car are negatively affected by those who do, and as a result they too become car users. Moreover, this behaviour is subsidised in various ways via the tax system. If you commute more than five kilometres by car to work, you can apply for a substantial tax reduction, but only if "the commuter gains two hours a day compared to travelling by public transport," which is rarely controlled by the tax authorities. Most parking spaces on municipal land in Swedish cities are today "free of charge", that is to say they are subsidised in order to make up for the absence of rental income.[124]

When car traffic increased explosively in Sweden in the 1950s, there was a six-fold increase in the number of retail parks and supermarkets.[125] The emergence of shopping centres outside the city is therefore a direct result of cars being the prevailing mode of transport. Without inexpensive cars, petrol and roads, there would be no shopping centres or retail parks. The day when petrol and cars become too expensive, retail parks will disappear. The fact is that many American shopping malls have seen some tough times lately. Studies show that a third of all American malls risk closure. Deadmalls.com contains an archive with pictures of ghost malls. However, the external retail market is an economic force to be reckoned with. The world's largest retail outlet in terms of revenue is the American Walmart with 2.2 million employees worldwide; the company's revenue in 2014 was 494 billion dollars.[127] The Swedish retail market showed a turnover of over 78 billion dollars and generated almost a quarter of a million jobs. Approximately thirty-five per cent comes from retail outlets outside of cities in Sweden, and the number of retail parks has steadily increased.[128] Retail outlets outside the city are dependent on people having access to cars and vice versa. This comes as no surprise, the less appealing the service and the more unpleasant high street shopping becomes due to traffic, the more attractive it is to do your shopping indoors at a shopping centre that not only drains the city centre, but even more so the smaller suburban commercial centres. Services are pulling out. This trend was intensified in the 1990s as retail parks started to sell clothes. The relationship between home and work is disintegrating. "There used to be an even distribution of services across town," says urban researcher Mats Franzén of the University of Uppsala. "Sweden is exceedingly generous towards those who promote urban sprawl. Our society is extremely adapted to cars, and the

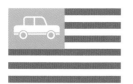

The automotive industry:

3%

or more of US GNP

peripheral districts were built for people with cars."

The automotive industry has been a driving force in the development of our car-based society. Henry Ford's mass produced cars paved the way for and the automotive industry in the United States and Europe were instrumental in promoting investments in more roads with less money allocated to public transport. "The Great American Streetcar Scandal" is an infamous and much discussed example of how General Motors systematically bought up and closed down rail services in the US.[130] By introducing legislation and national policies that favour public spending on road infrastructure, the Western world has gradually built up a society dependent on cars, which reproduces car consumers to the point where we are today when the automotive industry has become the linchpin of society. According to the American Auto Alliance,

> America's automotive industry is one of the largest industries in the country. The industry directly employs over 1.5 million people engaged in designing, engineering, manufacturing and supplying parts and components to assemble, sell and service new motor vehicles. America's automakers are among the largest purchasers of aluminum, copper, iron, lead, plastics, rubber, textiles, vinyl, steel and computer chips. When jobs from other sectors that are dependent on the industry are included, the auto industry is responsible for 7.25 million jobs nationwide, or about 3.8 percent of private-sector employment. The contribution of automotive manufacturing to compensation in the private sector is estimated at more than $500 billion each year. People in auto-related jobs collectively generate more than $205 billion annually in tax revenues. Historically, the auto industry has contributed from 3-3.5 percent to America's total gross domestic product.[131]

On their web site, the Bil Sweden car lobby organisation claims that,

> Sweden is among the countries in the world where the economy is most dependent on the automotive industry.

> Two world-leading bus and heavy vehicles manufacturers, Scania and Volvo, are Swedish [...] The industry's importance for jobs, ex-

An estimated

155

billion Swedish kronor (18 billion US dollars)

will be spent on state road maintenance in Sweden over the next ten years ports and dissemination of knowledge is great and, not least, it has an influence on commercial policy [...] The automotive industry employs approximately 110,000 Swedes and is responsible for 18 billion dollars in exports.[132]

When the financial magazine *Fortune* in 2015 listed the world's highest ranking companies in terms of revenue, two were car manufacturers, and Walmart was at the top of the list.[133] Anyone who questions the place of cars in society risks being accused of threatening jobs, welfare and growth, and rightly so.

No roads no cars. There are 98,500 kilometres of state-owned roads in Sweden. Over the next ten years, nearly 20 billion dollars of the taxpayers' money will be spent on the running and maintenance of these roads. A large chunk of the money goes to the major construction companies, which are completely dependent on road projects for their profit and survival. Some projects impose a greater economic burden on society than others, however. Sweden's most extensive road construction project ever, a seventeen-kilometre-long motorway tunnel in western Stockholm, is estimated to cost a minimum of four billion dollars, which corresponds to 125 new schools or 16,000 kilometres of cycle lanes. According to the Transport Administration's own figures, this is a viable and profitable project for society as a whole.[134] It is hard to understand why this is so, since the real estate and office markets are hardly affected by car access.[135] Moreover, extensive research has shown that more roads generate more traffic and more emissions.[136] After the opening of the Norra Länken bypass, traffic increased by six or seven per cent in Stockholm.[140] Another bypass project, Förbifart Stockholm, will reduce traffic that passes through central Stockholm, but according to the Traffic Administration's own figures, traffic flows on Essingeleden will be higher than today ten years after its completion. This is simply another motorway project that will increase car traffic, emissions and urban sprawl in Stockholm, a very antiquated infrastructure investment that will no doubt cost more than it is worth.

The National Road and Transport Research Institute (VTI) estimates that 120,000 people are working on road construction projects in Sweden today. Some are developers, some are employed at the City Traffic Administration and VTI and others at the many consultant companies and sub-contractors that are involved in the project. They would all like to do well, but they are also keen not to lose their jobs. Traffic planners produce sheaves of reports and data about car traffic and infrastructure every day. The Danish urban designer Jan Gehl often points out that this is one of the most fundamental problems associated with urban development. We produce a lot of data and knowledge about some issues, but we know far too little about others. We know very little about pedestrians, for example, about how much we walk in our cities and where to. So it is not only the physical infrastructure that generates car traffic, the institutional infrastructure – authorities, research teams and corporations that live off car traffic – is in fact generating a car-dependent society. Their *systemic world* has become our *lifeworld*, to paraphrase the philosopher Jürgen Habermas.[141]

I have participated in many lengthy discussions on the subject of cars with industry representatives as well as with friends. It is an emotional subject. What can be more deeply rooted in us than the way we live and our cars? The conversation often begins with a general discussion about car traffic and its devastating effects on the city and life in the city. Most people tend to agree, except perhaps the most inveterate car users. The average car user often expresses resignation – "But I have to use the car in order to sort out my daily life, what with driving the kids to pre-school, going shopping, travelling to work and back again." This is of course true. A lot of people are dependent on their car. Then the conversation often turns to where people live. If I claim that urban sprawl is the very reason for car dependence and congestion, the atmosphere tends to turn sour. During his lectures, the architect Jeff Speck use to show a picture of suburbia and ask his students, "If this is what you want …" Then he would show a picture of a motorway queue and say, "This is what you get!" No doubt most people know that this is true, but the fact that where we live affects closeness and distance to the city and forces us to travel in a certain way is a complex ethical dilemma.

City driving and ethics is difficult

My all-time favourite form of motion is the car. I'm one of those people. I love cars. It's the greatest physical object I've ever seen. I don't know why, really. My only theory is, when you're driving, you're outside and inside, moving and completely still, all at the same time. I think that's something.

The above quote is an excerpt from the stand-up comedian Jerry Seinfeld's book *Seinlanguage*.[142] Cars have created unparalleled mobility for individuals; they are status symbols that represent freedom, independence and success. "We got one last chance to make it real/To trade in these wings on some wheels [...] It's a town full of losers/And I'm pulling out of here to win," sang Bruce Springsteen in "Thunder Road" in 1976. The American word for "motorway" is "freeway". When a major car manufacturer recently launched a system for self-driving cars, they introduced it by claiming that it "has always been about freedom ... and it's still about freedom". According to sociologist Olle Hagman, a car can be thought of as a body extension, like a suit. It has become a part of us that (we believe) we cannot do without.[143] But if we look at all the disadvantages it is a suit that chafes. (The following information may cause discomfort in frequent drivers, but remember that cities built for cars were created by 20th century politicians, urban developers, lobbyists and engineers, not by drivers.)

Owning and driving a car costs around six hundred dollars a month. This includes fuel, repairs, depreciation, insurance, taxes, etc. Imagine that your rent suddenly goes up by six hundred dollars a month. That is a lot of money to some; in fact, fewer low-income earners, women, students, old age pensioners and immigrants own a car and travel less by car.[144]

In Sweden

70%

of all car journeys are made by men

" Traffic crashes is the most common cause of death for young people worlwide "

Seventy per cent of all motorists in Sweden are men.[145] An insurance company has compiled information on accidents involving pedestrians between 2000 and 2009 in Sweden, and it turned out that seventy-seven per cent of the drivers were men and sixty per cent of those that were hit by cars were women. Car-dependence is a contributing factor when it comes to gender and class inequality. When we invest our tax money in roads instead of public transport, we exacerbate this inequality. Some people are certainly aware of the fact that there is a cost, but few are likely to know exactly what it is. According to one estimate, parking spaces in the United States alone are subsidised by 310 billion dollars every year, which is five times the country's education budget.[147] Is parking more important than education? The hidden costs have proved to be astronomical. The World Resource Institute Embarq has estimated that congestion costs forty-three billion dollars a year in Rio de Janeiro and São Paulo, a figure that corresponds to eight per cent of the cities' GNP.[148] It is estimated that time wasted commuting by car to and from suburbs in the United States amounts to four hundred billion dollars a year.[149] A cursory estimation of how much car-dependence costs society in the United States shows that the total social cost – roads, health care, the environment, free parking, travel time, etc. – amounts to over three thousand billion dollars a year.[150]

Suburban sprawl generates a need for motorised transport, which presupposes access to vast land areas, forest and agricultural land. Scholars have estimated that cities in the next fifteen to twenty years will increase by over a million square kilometres worldwide, an area the size of South Africa that today largely consists of productive agricultural land and forest.[151] Car-based urban sprawl is thus a very real threat to the agriculture and forestry that sustain our cities. A large number of ecological studies indicate that roads disrupt ecosystems by cutting off dispersion routes and interfering with valuable natural assets.[152] One million mammals are killed on the roads every day in the United States alone; it is estimated that vehicle traffic, after the meat industry, is the greatest animal killer in the world.[153] Moreover, private lawns have a very real effect on water consumption. In the United States, the largest irrigated area of cultivated land consists of private lawns – they cover an area that is three times larger than all the country's corn plantations put together.[154] It seems obvious that the city suburbs and the road infrastructure associated with them are encroaching on our ecosystems.[155]

Roads also contribute to the segregation of neighbourhoods and individuals. According to a study by the American architect Donald Appleyard, the more traffic that passes on a street, the fewer contacts there are between neighbours that live on either side of that street.[156] Children can no longer run across to their neighbours as they have been doing for thousands of years. Everyone knows that people become injured and die as a cause of widespread car traffic, but few are aware of the figures – thirty-nine million people are injured and 1.2 million die annually across the world as a result of traffic.[157] Road accidents is the most common cause of death for young people worlwide.[158] For example, a third of those that were killed in traffic in Los Angeles were pedestrians.[159] According to a British study, children of low-income earners are twenty-eight times more likely to be killed in traffic than children from a wealthier background. That is to say, more people have died yearly as a cause of motorism than in all the wars in the world. It is estimated that two and a half million people will be killed by smog every year, which is intimately connected to car emissions. Several major cities have been forced to introduce radical traffic restrictions on account of air pollution. In Paris, Milan, Rome,[160] Delhi[161] and Beijing[162] acute measures have been taken through a system based on registration plates with a view to reducing car traffic by half. In China, where there are an estimated four thousand smog-related deaths every day,[163] they have started to sell canned Canadian air.[164] The estimated smog-related costs in Beijing are between seven and fifteen per cent of the city's GNP.[165]

A research team at the University of Umeå have discovered that the risk for people who live in heavily polluted streets of developing Alzheimer's disease and dementia is higher than for people who live in places where the air is cleaner. One of the researchers, Bertil Forsberg, reports that,

> Sixteen per cent of all dementia cases included in the study may be attributable to exhaust fume exposure […] the risk of developing Alzheimer or vascular dementia for the twenty-five per cent that were exposed to the highest levels at their home was approximately forty per cent compared to the twenty-five per cent exposed to the lowest level.[166]

According to an American study, elderly people who live in highly polluted environments experience lower blood circulation in the brain and are more at risk of developing dementia. Tiny particles can reach the brain via the olfactory nerve and cause damage there. Exhaust fumes have also been shown to cause inflammation of the respiratory tract and other organs, which, among other things, may affect blood circulation in the brain, according to Bertil Forsberg.

As everyone knows, car traffic generates noise, which causes a depreciation of housing – especially in detached housing areas – of up to thirty per cent.[167] Other negative effects include insomnia and psychological problems.[168] While people who live in cities are often healthier,[169] a large number of medical studies show that lack of exercise and car dependence have a major role in the current obesity epidemic. In the 1970s, one of ten Americans was overweight, now it is one in three.[170] Obesity causes a higher incidence of cardiovascular disease. People that live in dense city districts where they can access most services by foot are only half as likely to become overweight.[171] It may sound contradictory, but having a grocery store within walking distance, the risk of being overweight is reduced by eleven per cent, ostensibly on account of less car travel. A Swedish study confirms that physical activity is higher and that people move around more in dense city districts where you can access services by foot.[172] Experts recommend that you walk for at least thirty minutes every day, preferably in the morning.[173] Consequently, those who do not walk or cycle, but use their car to get to work every day should add thirty minutes to their commuting time in order to stay healthy. Urban sprawl causes stress and health problems.

Transportation of people and goods generate up to twenty -five per cent of all climate changing carbon emissions; half comes from private cars.[174] According to one calculation, the ecological footprint caused by fuel and materials is approximately eight hundred times the surface of the car itself, which is ten square metres.[175] It means that one single car requires eight thousand square metres, or the surface of eight hundred cars. In a world where we are looking at three billion cars in 2050, their combined footprint will amount to twenty-four million square kilometres, or sixteen per cent of the earth's surface. It has been made clear that the automotive industry is finding the emissions problem hard to master after Volkswagen was found to have manipulated emissions tests for eleven million cars.[176] The scandal reverberated throughout the industry. The term "eco-car" is by no means uncomplicated. The recently introduced term "super eco-car" is tragicomic. The ambivalence of the industry is obvious when you look at the advertising campaigns in which they try to outsmart each other in eco-friendliness, often with the help of celebrities. Most brands have stopped showing cars in urban environments; these days they are associated with wilderness and a virgin natural landscape, most likely in order to give associations of freedom of movement and nature, but perhaps also because car manufacturers have come to realise that cars do not fit well into the urban environment. If you are selling a car to people living in a city you do not want to show how it destroys their neighbourhood and even causes problems for their fellow citizens.

> Cars have always been a symbol of freedom. Today, that freedom is being challenged by the heavy and unpredictable traffic commuters are forced to endure. At car manufacturer X, we believe autonomous driving will recapture this freedom, allowing drivers to choose how every moment in the car is spent. [177]

In the light of the above quote, driving a car is presented as individualistic, almost antisocial and as something that has serious effects on society as a whole. The word antisocial may sound a little harsh, but a new study shows that people who drive a lot have a more negative view of people outside the car, especially when they are younger or have a lower socio-economic status.[178]

> When in my car I get a different set of values. I'm the worst person I can be when I'm behind the wheel, which is when I'm at my most dangerous. When you're driving that's when you need to be the most compassionate and responsible in any time of your life because you are fucking driving a WEAPON.

This is how the stand-up comedian Louis CK describes his own shortcomings as a driver.[179] So the people who drive the cars become isolated too. According to a recently published study, people that commute by car have less social capital, they socialise less and they trust others less than people who walk, cycle or travel to work by public transport.[180]

If the city is the great forum for social interaction, having people isolated inside cars becomes a problem – it interferes with people's quality of life. There is an ethical issue here, which is similar to a problem that in game theory is referred to as the prisoner's dilemma[181] whereby two prisoners locked in two different cells have more to gain by blaming each other, even if they would both be released if they did not. They only risk the longest sentence if one of the prisoners blames the other. It shows the risk of acting only for your own benefit without consulting others, thus forcing them to accept a less advantageous solution. This is how motorists behave. As soon as one begins to drive – the children to school, for example – their driving becomes a risk for the children that are walking to school, so their parents begin to drive their children to school too. If one drives everyone drives. This is a problem that is very real in front of school entrances today. However, if parents all agree that all children have to walk to school everyone benefits.

A friend of mine told me that every day when he accompanied his child to school on foot he would walk past one of his neighbours whose child went to the same school. The neighbour drove his child in his car; my friend walked or cycled. They greeted each other in the street every morning, but the whole situation was a little strange because they often met up near the school entrance fifteen minutes later. One day my friend asked his neighbour if he would be prepared to give his child a lift because it is, after all, practical to share. The neigh-bour agreed, and my friend's child got a lift to school every morning. After a couple of weeks the neighbour informed my friend that he could not do it anymore since he did not have a spare safety seat. The neighbour did not want to put my friend's child at risk in case of an accident. So my friend went back to walking or cycling with his child to school while the neighbour's child was driven in a (safety-rated) car in a (safety-rated) car seat. Now the two children pass each other on their way to school, one inside a car and the other on foot, and the life of my friend's child depends on whether his neighbour stops in front of the pedestrian crossing. The road to hell is certainly paved with good intentions. The car society has made it hard to co-operate on equal terms.

In spring 2015, the City of Stockholm decided to close Swedenborgsgatan in South Stockholm to car traffic over the summer months. The debate that followed shows how controversial an issue this is, especially when it comes to defending children's way of life. "Ola" writes,

> How do they imagine that we who live here should drive our young children home before we spend half an hour looking for a parking space. Will we not be allowed to pack and unpack our cars, no one will be able to move [...] I guess that the people who are suggesting this do not live here, or drive, or have children. We are trying to raise a family here in this stressful, demanding society for the sake of our children, but now this is going to be made more difficult, and we have lived here since 1992.

"Göran" replies,

> This is a great idea [the pedestrian precinct], many children live in the city centre, the cars pollute the air they breathe and limit their movements. There is plenty of public transport compared to other cities. They should do the same on Götgatan, it is not sensible that we who pay millions for our homes should have to jostle with people on pavements that offer free euthanasia should we happen to take one step into a road that is used by aggressive motorists from other parts of town.

"Söderbönan" says,

> The most important and valuable deliveries are those of children, the disabled and the elderly who need to get home. We who live on Swedenborgsgatan drive our children to various sport activities in inaccessible sports centres far out of town. Then you have to try and find a parking space late at night. If the road is closed to vehicles it will not only become impossible to drive children to and from home, and a large number of parking spaces will disappear.[182]

After the trial the shops and restaurants along the street were asked to comment on their experience. One restaurant reported that their turnover had gone up by twenty per cent.[183]

Car users are "freeriders" in economic terms, [184] that is to say people who are using a system at the expense of others and who force others to use an imperfect system. The more people

Each time you opt out of travelling through town by car you contribute the following:

Better road safety and reduced risk of human injury and death, especially when it comes to children, the elderly and the disabled.

Better social integration by participating and being seen in public spaces as well as pulling down barriers between neighbourhoods.

Improved health and fitness. It reduces the risk of cardiovascular disease, which in turn reduces society's cost for health care.

Better accessibility for emergency services, buses, bikes, deliveries and disabled people who need to travel by car.

Improving your personal finances by lowering costs for fuel and maintenance.

Reducing society's expenditure for road and street maintenance.

Improving air quality by reducing emissions of toxic particles to the air and exhaust fumes that cause acidification of soil and water.

Higher real estate values, especially for housing, as well as better turnover for shops at street level.

Reducing carbon dioxide and other greenhouse gas emissions that contribute to climate change.

Reducing the risk of animals being injured and killed in traffic and thereby contributing to biological diversity.

Reducing noise levels, which leads to a quieter city and better mental health and wellbeing for the citizens.

Showing family, friends, co-workers and fellow human beings that it is possible to live without a car.

that drive, the worse the environment for those who do not becomes. This is why the demand for suburbs is growing in cities. When the car-dependent suburban population drive their cars into central town, they make it so unattractive that those who live there choose to move out to the suburbs (if they can) to a life dependent on using a car. If everyone agreed not to drive everywhere, but to walk and cycle instead there would be less traffic, there would be more space to build new parks and playgrounds and more people, especially families with children, would chose to continue to live in the city centre.

We are stuck with a system psychologists call "choice blindness".[185] We believe that we "choose" to drive cars, but it is in fact the system, that is to say the structure of the city and the transport on offer, that has made the choice for us and that forces us to become dependent on cars. Who, really, wants to clutch at a steering wheel while staring into someone else's bumper day after day? What kind of life is that, being stuck inside a tin box? Is urbanization all about people desiring more than anything to sit in cars, or is it the other way around, because they want to get away from it and get a better social life? Why are we accepting, in a society where human value is paramount, to put our lives at risk every time we step into the street? How can we not see the enormous blow that has been dealt to our cities during the course of the 20th century and the damages that motorism inflicts on humans and society every day? We do not see it because the physical (roads, pavements, sprawl) and institutional (legislation, authorities, corporations) structures choose it for us.

Consider the most basic of all ethical principles: when you do something for your own benefit it can never affect others negatively. Do we keep this in mind when we get behind the wheel in a densely developed area? As soon as you step on the accelerator and turn into the street you may injure and kill people with your tin suit. They only need to look a little too long at their mobile phone and stray a couple of steps into the street. If you are driving at forty kilometres per hour, there is a fifty per cent risk that the person you hit will die.[186] If you do an Internet search for "car crashes involving pedestrians" an occurrence that may feel extremely unlikely suddenly becomes very real and unpleasant. It is violent, brutal and uncivilised. "We have two serious public health issues in this country," said San Francisco's traffic commissioner, Ed Reiskin, at the Designing Cities conference in Austin in 2015, "gun violence and traffic violence". Today, the number of people who are shot and killed and the number of people who are killed in traffic is the same in the United States.[187] Twice as many died in traffic compared to gun violence in the 1980s. Comparing cars and guns, like the stand-up comedian Louis CK did, may seem a little over the top, but it is not too far off the mark. Both cars and guns are artefacts that we humans have access to and that we can use to kill others, either deliberately or by accident. The American National Rifle Association (NRA) often claims that "weapons don't kill people, people kill people".[188] It makes me think of another stand-up comedian, Eddie Izzard, who commented on the slogan by saying, "They (NRA) say that guns don't kill people, people kill people. I think the gun helps. If you just stood there and yelled BANG I don't think you'd kill too many people." [189] According to a recent study, drivers are distracted by phone calls, texting, mobile surfing, music, conversations et cetera more than half the time they are driving.[190] Even though car dependence cannot be ultimately blamed on drivers, but on 20th century politicians, lobbyists and developers, people who are able to walk, cycle or use public transport and still drive must have some kind of moral responsibility?

Let us consider the following thought experiment. What would happen if we made drivers and pedestrians equal? Turning the exhaust pipe so the exhaust fumes are released into the car would radically contaminate the air inside the vehicle, but it would not instill a fear of pedestrians. Respect for pedestrians and other road users would, on the other hand, be greater if we installed a "steelbag" that would be released when a car crashes into an unprotected road user. (Please note that this is of course

Traffic accidents are caused by dangerous streets and unsafe drivers. They are not accidents. Let's stop using the word "accident" today

simply a theoretical construction and not a serious suggestion.) Contrary to an airbag, the steelbag, would knock the driver as hard as it knocks the pedestrian it hits. Driving with a steelbag would make drivers much more careful and other road users safer. It would work like a reverse prisoner's dilemma. However, it does not solve the problem parents experience when they are walking with their children along a busy street. Children are impulsive and may rush into the road without warning. How can we give a parent who is driving with a child in the car the same experience? Perhaps by removing the bodywork and let the child sit on an ordinary chair without a seatbelt and with its own steering wheel that it now and then uses to steer the car.

Families for Safe Streets is a New York association for people who have lost a family member in traffic. Many are parents whose children were killed by reckless drivers or by people who were driving under the influence of alcohol or drugs. They are affiliated with the non-profit organisation Transportation Alternatives, promoting safer pedestrian, cycle and public transport in their city. Families for Safe Streets have, among other things, succeeded in reducing the speed limit in New York from fifty to forty kilometres an hour (30–25 miles/hour) and persuaded the city council to endorse a zero vision based on the zero vision that was introduced in Sweden in 1997. "The fundamental message of Vision Zero is that death and injury on city streets is not acceptable, and that we will no longer regard serious crashes as inevitable," says the Mayor of New York, Bill de Blasio, on the city's web site.

This success was preceded by some serious lobbying according to Caroline Samponaro, assistant director at Transportation Alternatives.[191] She, and many with her, are not aware of the fact that the Swedish zero vision was not put in place to save pedestrians and cyclists. Its chief purpose was to increase road safety in order to save drivers' lives. It is remarkable that the Swedish zero vision shows so little concern for the safety of pedestrians and cyclists. It hardly makes a difference, says Caroline Samponaro. The Vision Zero concept has already spread and is having a major positive impact in several other American cities. Mayor de Blasio uses the word "crash" deliberately. Government agencies and the media have long used the term "road accident", but this is not entirely uncontroversial, according to Samponaro. It is a term that fails to take the driver's responsibility, the person that may be responsible for injury and death, into account. It is derived from the way cars have come to dominate over the past hundred years and the current hegemony of the car. For that reason, Transportation Alternatives' most recent campaign was named *Crash Not Accident* and its purpose is to change people's perception from "road accidents" to "car crashes". The following quote can be found on their web site.

> Planes don't have accidents. They crash. Cranes don't have accidents. They collapse. And as a society we expect answers and solutions. Traffic accidents are fixable solutions, caused by dangerous streets and unsafe drivers. They are not accidents. Let's stop using the word "accident" today.[192]

Caroline Samponaro says that Families for Safe Streets are spearheading this work. This is no leisure society, these are parents whose children have been killed in traffic and who demand a more equal, safer city environment.

These are some of the questions posed: When it comes to equality, is it reasonable to allow someone who can afford a car to threaten to kill a person who does not? Is it reasonable for parents to be afraid that their children might be killed on the streets? Is it at all reasonable to live under this threat every day of your life? Why are cars not fitted with GPS systems that issue a fine as soon as a driver exceeds the speed limit? Why are pedestrians not in control of traffic lights? Why are the penalties for traffic offences so lenient? Why is there no government warning on car advertisements as there is for cigarettes? According to Enrique Peñalosa, these inequalities are just as absurd as the fact that women were not allowed to vote a hundred years ago. A lot of people at the time did not think it unfair, just as most of us have for a long time failed to open our eyes to the hegemony of the car. Whether "peak car" exists or not is beside the point. It is as irrelevant as discussing whether we have achieved "peak gun". A radical reduction in car traffic in our cities is absolutely crucial, especially in terms of bringing people closer together. People are increasingly beginning to understand this, and some major changes are under way.

Mike Lydon, urban designer and author of the book *Tactical Urbanism,* explains why. "Some people think it's radical to take away cars from city streets, but I think it's much more radical to promote death and destruction with tax payers money."[193]

WHAT IS HAPPENING?

It all begins with activism

Ever since cars first began to occupy city streets, local opposition has manifested itself. A strong opposition was beginning to come to the fore as early as in the 1920s.[194] The first organised action on record took place 1955 in San Francisco when plans for new freeways through the city were made public. Because of the protests, several so-called alignments were shelved, but the Embarcadero Freeway along San Francisco's shoreline was constructed despite opposition, leading to subsequent demolition and conversion to a city street in 1989.[195] Jane Jacob's struggle against the freeway developer Robert Moses led to her arrest, and a planned freeway on Lower Manhattan was blocked. This event is considered a milestone for activists and urbanists.

At about the same time in Stockholm, the city council decided to cut down thirteen elm trees to make way for a metro station in the Kungsträdgården public park. People had become fed up with the all the demolition and the road construction projects that were disrupting the city centre. The elm trees were eventually saved after a great deal of tumult, and the entrance to the metro was moved a few hundred metres. The protest actions were organised by the Alternativ stad (alternative city) movement that had been formed two years earlier, in 1969, by some committed architecture students, activists and other city huggers.[196] What they fought for was,

> A city for people to live in, a city developed not only for cars and office complexes, a city in which you can move safely without damaging the environment, a city with more parks and public places for everyone to enjoy, a city that grows in a controlled manner with human needs and proportions in mind.[197]

Alternativ stad was among the first to organise a Reclaim the Streets action. On August 24, 1969, which was Children's Day, a group of activists barricaded the roundabout on Sergels torg and put up a streamer that read "No cars 365 days a year". The police intervened. Since then, the movement has carried out a large number of similar actions where participants sit down in the street without previous warning or organise street parties. Alternativ stad was also involved in an international traffic revolution, a unified action against cars in the streets of Stockholm, Amsterdam, London and New York. In central Stockholm, they "occupied" a parking lot at Fridhemsplan. This was a completely legal demonstration. As soon as a parking space became free, they placed a bicycle on it and paid the fee while they served coffee and buns to passers-by. In early 1972, when Alternativ stad was at its most active, many other action groups, so-called village councils, operated in central Stockholm, fighting the onslaught of traffic and construction of new motorways.[198] A cycle faction within Alternativ stad organised cycling demonstrations for a car-free city centre. One of them was led by the French film director Jaques Tati who was in Stockholm to promote his new film *Traffic*. In 1972, the group began to lend second-hand bikes to the public, "the white bicycles", based on a Dutch idea.[199]

There was also a tree faction within Alternativ stad. It was formed in order to conduct a tree-planting scheme that had been approved by the city council, but never implemented. Their mission was to plant trees, but they were stopped by police.

One of the organisation's most important actions took place in 1993 when nearly 5,000 people marched through central Stockholm in protest against the extensive increase in motorways that was included in a political bid referred to as "Dennispaketet". Alternativ stad was well ahead of its time in the way the organisation took physical space away from cars in a peaceful and festive spirit.[200]

Planka.nu is an organisation that is in some ways similar to Alternativ stad. They are persistently trying to change the way the general public and politicians look at public transport and motorism, among other things through the book *Trafik-maktordningen* (the traffic power structure) and the *Planka.fm* podcast. The organisation demands free public transport, and they have attracted the attention of the media by actively encouraging people to freeride. The following can be found on their web site.

> You simply cannot compromise when it comes to public transport. It is the central nervous system of the city and a common concern, a precondition for the economic and social life of the city. The cost we pay for public transport is a structural problem, but also a real problem for individual citizens. It is not fair that a millionaire and an unemployed person should pay the same for using public transport. State-financed, free public transport would mean that each individual pays according to his or her means. [201]

In the book, they offer strong and convincing supporting evidence for saying that planning for cars is not the way forward.

> The traffic power structure is a systemic transport hierarchy with the car at the top and public transport, pedestrians and cyclists at the bottom. As a result, these means of transport are not allocated the same amount of space. As the car is at the top of the hierarchy, society becomes based on automobile transportation. A world in which our lives are too dependent on cars [...] Motorism divides us. Most of us know what it feels like to get behind the wheel and find that you have suddenly become a Driver. Driving seems to automatically turn people into egoists that try to achieve something at the ex-

The traffic power structure is a systemic transport hierarchy with the car at the top and public transport, pedestrians and cyclists at the bottom.

pense of others. When you're behind the wheel everyone else (other drivers, cyclists, pedestrians, public transport users) is by definition an obstacle. Who cannot truly confess to having experienced the aggressive, competitive, selfish behaviour of a car user?

Just like Alternativ stad, Planka.nu strongly opposes major motorway projects, most recently the Förbifart Stockholm bypass.

They [the politicians] claim that it is necessary, unavoidable, the only way to go. But this is not true. It is in fact extremely complicated to try and persuade people in a city of a million people to travel by car. It is like trying to get as many people as possible to use Segways. They take up a lot of space, they are extremely expensive and people get hurt. Not to mention how stupid they look. There is no reason why we should finance more cars, more emissions and less space for people. We can choose what we would like Stockholm to be; without new roads there will not be more cars. Free public transport and more public transport services are alternative solutions.[202]

Planka.nu stands out as a group of young citizens that unlike Alternativ stad focus not only on a car-free city centre, they also fight for the ability to live in the suburbs without a car as well as free public transport for all.

Reclaim the Streets appears to have started in London where

the organisation in 1991 opposed the building of new roads by occupying streets and blocking traffic. The movement soon spread with actions in Europe as well as in Australia and the United States. Most of these actions were carried out between 1995 and 2002. To begin with, focus was on criticising car traffic, but the demonstrations became increasingly anti-capitalist. In Sweden, the movement was referred to as Reclaim the City. Reclaim the City demonstrations organised by Gatans parlament (the parliament of the street) in Stockholm led to several instances of public disturbance as well as vandalised cars and shops. Over two hundred people were arrested at a demonstration on Götgatan.[203] Street parties turned into riots. Reclaim has since gone over to other forms of activism, like the Occupy movement, which spread quickly across the world. Occupy Wall Street started in 2011 in Zyccotti Park, a park on private land on Manhattan, as a general protest against capitalism and the banking system. I visited their camp, and like the Reclaim demonstration it was much like a street party, even including a samba orchestra. Occupy reached Stockholm too, where a small camp was pitched on Brunkebergstorg in central town.

Regardless of whom these movements are targeting, it is interesting to see that people who want to change society do so in public places, as in the above-mentioned elm protests or the Arabian Spring. It is particularly interesting to note that Tahrir Square in Cairo is not a square in the traditional sense of the word, but a large roundabout where protesters blocked traffic. It is only logical that criticism of the status quo includes the way cars move in public space. Occasionally, inner city riots – like Reclaim the City – or riots that occur in the suburbs – as in Rosengård in Malmö or Husby in Stockholm – result in vandalised and burning cars. Parked cars occupy public space in a way that no other private property does and are thereby very tangible symbols of economic inequality.

Other, less confrontational movements also make their mark on public space. It is a phenomenon known as do-it-yourself-urbanism or tactical urbanism.[204] Various groups start projects with the aim of converting the city into a more social, meaningful place to be. In their book *Tactical Urbanism,* Mike Lydon and Anthony Garcia say that it is a bit like hacking into the urban systems, stimulating change by finding loopholes and cracks.[205]

Guerrilla gardening started when a group of activists threw condoms filled with seeds, water and fertilizer onto derelict plots in New York. They wanted to show that abandoned city environments could be used for something and improved. These allotments are also part of a wider social project. The first occupied guerrilla garden – established by the Green Guerrillas in 1973 in New York – was so popular that it is now maintained by the city's parks department. [206] In Portland, seven hundred volunteers have broken up almost ten thousand square metres of asphalt in order to plant grass, flowers and bushes through the Depave movement. In southern Stockholm, a garden has been planted on some old, disused railway tracks by the organisation Trädgård på spåret (garden on the tracks).[207] The area has become a meeting place for garden enthusiasts and has brought to life an area that would otherwise have been perceived as dark and unsafe. The organisation has teamed up with the Trädgården nightclub, under the Skanstull Bridge where they use the space between the rails in a way that has brought the place to life, leading to an increase in land value. Property developers will soon be queuing up to develop this attractive area.

The activity of putting chairs out on the street is called chair-bombing. When the City of San Francisco in 2011 passed a law that prevented people from sitting or lying on the pavement, the DoTank activist group organised an action in which they put out groups of simple, home-made chairs across the city. Some were so popular that they became permanent fixtures. I initiated a similar project in Stockholm together with city enthusiasts Lars Strömgren and Paul Alarcon. Our plan was to place out one hundred painted benches along Götgatan in Stockholm. We called the project SOFA (because Götgatan borders on to the Sofo district south of Folkungagatan). The City had just removed two lanes on Götgatan, parking spaces had been moved further out into the street and cycle lanes and pavements had been widened. The municipality called it an investment in cycling zones, but we thought that street-life could be improved too. In our proposal, the benches would be decorated by members of the local community: residents, schools and art associations. They were to build a two-kilometre-long art bench exhibition that would give the place some local colour while at the same time offering passers-by a place to sit down. We contacted the Swedish Property Federation who liked the idea and were happy to sponsor the seats. We now had financial backing and were ready to go. A few weeks earlier, the city council had endorsed a plan for supporting local initiatives, so when the civil servants at the traffic department showed some doubt about the project, we asked the politicians instead. The then traffic commissioner replied that the project was in violation of the city's graffiti policy! We were all taken-aback; it must have been part of some political gambit. Even though the time was right the project failed, despite the fact that the media were reporting on food trucks and open street projects, and our project had financial backing and an organisation to implement it.

During the Citymoves conference in Stockholm in 2015, parklets, or pop-up parks, were planned in order to showcase how the streetspace can be used and altered. Happy Sweden is an organisation that studies the influence of citizens, minor associations, et cetera. They filed an application for placing some picnic chairs on a parking space for a period of three hours. This turned out to be a major undertaking since the following is required. A permit issued by the police that costs one hundred dollars; a plan including all measurements has to be submitted with the application. The police then forward the application to the City Traffic Administration and any other relevant bodies. The Traffic Administration in turn requires a plan for how traffic will be affected. This plan has to be produced by an independent consultant for a fee. The Municipality then approves the plan, which costs 225 dollars. Moreover, to use a parking space along a street requires placing a concrete block at either end so cars cannot access the parklet. Rental and transportation of these concrete blocks costs in excess of 375 dollars. Add to that costs for any signage that needs to be adapted. The Traffic Administration also charges a fee of between fourteen and twenty dollars per square metre a day for the use of public land, that is to say about 190 dollars a day. The total cost of placing two picnic chairs on a parking space for two hours would amount to a minimum of 1,125 dollars and an application period of two to three months.

A permit does not guarantee that the parklet will take place, however. Should a car park illegally in the space that you have rented you cannot demand that it be moved, as the Traffic Administration does not consider it to be parked in such a way that it obstructs traffic. As a result, Happy Sweden chose a different strategy. They decided that they would do like the strip clubs and put their business on wheels. They placed the picnic chairs on a trailer, delivered the trailer to a parking space and paid the fee. It was now a legal parklet because it had wheels.[208] This is an interesting example of the power of traffic, the fact that laws and regulations that apply in public space give precedence to private cars instead of human activity. It shows the inertia of change within the legal spectrum; you need imagination and a good strategy to succeed.

The next step is tactical

Pallis on Åsögatan in southern Stockholm was a pop-up park that appeared during the Citymoves conference. It was a collaboration between the Property Federation, Sweden's largest architecture firm, White, and a local resident who just happened to be the famous comedian Måns Herngren. This project succeeded due to a wide contact network as well as plenty of social and economic backing, but it was not easy and it involved a lot of unpaid effort. One trick to make the council process the application faster was to define the park as a "religious gathering", which it was not of course, even if the result, when the park was finally in place, was a kind of existential milestone.

Parks have been used for activism before. The landscape architect and artist Bonnie Ora Sherk carried out the art project Portable Parks in several abandoned traffic spaces in San Francisco in 1970. It was a precursor of the modern-day parklets and the annual event PARK(ing) Day.[209] In its most basic form, a parklet is a parking space with grass, tables and chairs. A trend was born when the design company Rebar turned a parking lot into a pocket park in 2005. Just like Alternativ stad in Stockholm, Rebar paid the parking fee and posted a sign, inviting people to put some coins into the parking meter if they liked the park.

This was an inspiration to others. PARK(ing) Day takes place around the world every year on the third Friday of September. In 2011, 975 Parklets were organised in 165 cities in thirty-five countries. Today, the San Francisco Planning Department has produced a manual as an aid for local groups when they build their parklets. The city has also initiated a Pavement to Parks programme, which has inspired over fifty new parklet developments in San Francisco.

Build a Better Block was started by a group of activists in Oak Cliff, Dallas. They wanted to interest local residents and property owners in opening up activities in ground floor premises in order to liven up the drab street environment. Food trucks, café tables and potted plants were placed on the street, cycle lanes were marked up and parking spaces removed. Build a Better Block is a small-scale initiative that has spread to other cities since its inception. PARK(ing) Day and Build a Better Block are example of how successful grassroots activism can turn into organised movements that support change and development in our cities.

The Open Street phenomenon has grown rapidly in the last few years. An open street or road is closed off for traffic during a limited period, normally by the local traffic department. This is not pure activism, even though the initiative may be taken by a non-profit organisation. The first Open Street was probably Seattle Bicycle Sundays in 1965, but the event that has caused the greatest attention is Bogotá's Ciclovía. In the early 1980s, the city closed a 120-kilometre road stretch every Sunday and bank holiday. Today, it is estimated that approximately two million people use the city's car-free zones when they are open to pedestrians and cyclists. Open Street has spread to Latin America, Australia and the United States. In 2015, 130 Open Street events were registered in the United States alone.[210] These include CicLAvia (Los Angeles), Long Beach Bike Festival, San Francisco Sunday Streets, Summer Streets (New York), Sunday Streets Berkeley, Bike Miami Days, Atlanta Streets Alive, Cyclovía Hawaii, Portland Sunday Parkways and Viva Streets Austin. CicLAvia in the infamous car city of Los Angeles is today one of the largest open street events in the world, and it began as a grassroots movement. The fist CicLAvia was held in 2010; ten kilometres of road was closed in 2014. Summer Street in New York means that all of Lafayette Street and Park Avenue, eleven kilometres of road, are closed for three days and filled with playgrounds, sports grounds, dance happenings, yoga and tai-chi classes, concerts and art installations. You have to remember that these are main thoroughfares.

In Europe, the EU-led campaigns In Town without My Car[211] and European Mobility Week[212] (usually at the end of September) have led to a number of temporary road closures since 1989. Over two thousand cities in forty-five countries participate every year. In 2015, more than nine hundred cities temporarily closed roads for vehicle traffic in one way or another, or instituted a car-free day.[213] Europe has a long tradition of street demonstrations on, for example, May 1. Now roads are closed not primarily for demonstrations, but for creating a better environment and to make them more attractive. In May 2010, the Champs-Élysées in Paris was closed to cars and converted to park areas and allotments. Images from the event make you think of a lush landscape that is more in line with the street's name, "the Elysean Fields", the land of paradise and eternal spring as it is described in Greek and Roman mythology. In the summer of 2013, Regent Street in London was closed over the course of four Sundays, which led to increased social interaction and commerce.[214]

In Stockholm, large areas have been closed to traffic during festivals on a number of occasions. The Water Festival of the 1990s showed that pedestrian precincts where people move about and share culture, food and drink is much more fun than streets with cars. It was an Open Street event even if it was not called that at the time. It may have been phased out because it became too commercial and thereby less popular. A public event has to be open and multi-faceted. If it is dominated by obvious commercial interests, it becomes pointless. It is therefore fundamental to an Open Street event that it is shared among cultures, as the Stockholm culture festival and the 08 Festival proved. The Open Street events that took place on Götgatan and Nytorget in 2013 and 2014 were smaller in scale, but got just as much attention since the city council closed several major roads. Open Street on Götgatan was part of a major conversion in which car lanes were removed, parking spaces were transferred to the street and cycle lanes and pavements were widened. Testing simple, inexpensive changes that are easily reversed in case they do not work out is called tactical urbanism; these are easier for the public to accept. Maybe this is worth a try?

In London and New York, local resident groups together with the Traffic Department, co-operate on a project called Play

Street. The City closes a road for traffic, often near a school or pre-school, for a period of time and organises play areas. Over half of the residents along the street must vote in favour of the Play Street for it to be implemented. In Jackson Heights, New York, the City has extended its closures to make this an annual event. These projects are extremely popular, so car-free streets where children are able to play like they did a hundred years ago may become a permanent fixture.

The most spectacular urban tactical project took place in Manhattan. The idea was simple. Times Square was closed off overnight using only concrete blocks and paint. The response was immediate. Janette Sadik-Khan recounts,

> It was like a Star Trek episode, you know? They weren't there before, and then zzzzzt! All the people arrived. Where they'd been, I don't know, but they were there. And this actually posed an immediate challenge for us, because the street furniture had not yet arrived. So we went to a hardware store and bought hundreds of lawn chairs, and we put those lawn chairs out on the street. And the lawn chairs became the talk of the town. It wasn't about that we'd closed Broadway to cars. It was about those lawn chairs.[215]

It was simple, inexpensive and popular, there was a radical reduction in the number of car crashes, more people moved around the streets and commerce was thriving. Times Square is now ranked as one of the world's best shopping destinations. [216] The project was completed in 2015 when a permanent solution designed by the Norwegian architectural firm Snøhetta was introduced. Snøhetta famously designed the Oslo opera house and the new library in Alexandria. Removing private car traffic is clearly an effective market strategy.

The development of Times Square from temporary traffic closures to a redeveloped pedestrian open space is a milestone. According to architect Mike Lydon, the term "tactical urbanism" comes from this project in which the city council was instrumental in transforming the area in cooperation with property owners and local organisations.[217] As early as in 2003, the property owners' association Times Square Alliance commissioned the two organisations Transportation Alternatives and Project for Public Spaces (PPS) to study pedestrian flows in Times Square. PPS filmed and charted flows, and pointed out how crowded the area was and the lack of spaces for simply hanging around. It was in fact so crowded that people constantly had to keep moving. Jan Gehl was also asked to study the area, and he confirmed the lack of pedestrian space, which was instead used for cars.[218]

Methods for systematically studying city life and what goes on in public spaces were developed by the anthropologist William H. Whyte in New York. Whyte and PPS's founder, the anthropologist Fred Kent, conducted the organisation's pioneering project, Bryant Park,[219] a small park in Midtown Manhattan, which was mostly visited by addicts and criminals in the 1980s. Where earlier strategies had involved greater security and surveillance and making the place unattractive, Whyte's solution instead made it more attractive with visitors, coffee shops and events. Bryant Park was redesigned and access to surrounding streets opened up with the assumption that "undesirable" visitors cannot be deterred and that they are part of city life. "So-called 'undesirables' are not the problem. It is the measures taken to combat them that is the problem," says Whyte.[220] If a lot of people are using the space, undesirable elements are a minority and everyone feels seen and safe. Not only did the park become a popular space with many visitors, the price of property around the park rose more than in the rest of Manhattan.

Project for Public Spaces represents a form of organised activism that started in small-scale neighbourhood projects and experimental research, and that have developed into an urban space development institution backed by UN Habitat and others. To reclaim space and use public space as a starting point for urban development, thereby bringing people closer together, has become increasingly uncontroversial, and contemporary urban planners are leading the way.

Urban planners are leading the way

Those who follow developments within urban planning can hardly have missed that there has been a shift in values. Jane Jacobs was among the most vocal critics of the large-scale modernist cities that were adapted for car traffic in the United States as early as in the 1960s. The opinions she raised intensified in Sweden in the 1970s as the large-scale housing projects known as the "million programme" were being implemented. Housing projects designed in the 1980s were already radically different, having gone from tower blocks and slab blocks surrounded by green areas to more city-like housing with blocks laid out in a street grid. The neo-urbanism that came to the fore in the United States in the 1980s, and which was formulated in the *Charter of New Urbanism* in 1993, served as inspiration for many developers. During the early period of Swedish modernism (1930–1960), traffic was usually integrated, with cars and pedestrians sharing the same street-space. After the introduction of the SCAFT planning guidelines in 1968, different types of road users were separated, so pedestrians were able to move around without having to cross busy roads. Different functions – housing, workplaces, services – became increasingly separate from one another. In the 1980s and '90s, critics reacted to the fact that these environments did not function like old neighbourhoods where the traffic was integrated. These old neighbourhoods were suddenly becoming more attractive and in greater demand. The often neglected inner cities were restored, and demand for central housing increased. The modernist credo, "more light, more air" was becoming less important to the urban developers that grew up at the end of the 20th century. If you look at the inflated property prices and the long queues for rented apartments that are legion in city centres today, it seems that the urbanists were right. The supply of urban assets cannot meet the demand. This is sometimes expressed as "lack of city".[221]

The traffic separation and road safety measures that were introduced in SCAFT, meant that the central area of the hou-

It is pedestrians, not cars, that drive the economy

sing programmes was car-free, a feature often appreciated by residents. Some municipalities have tried to remove pedestrian overpasses and integrate traffic, for example in Husby, but residents have protested against them. The possibility to walk from the metro to the shops and to school without encountering cars is preferable to having to cross busy roads. Many of the integrated housing projects in Stockholm (Dalen, Minneberg, Rissne) that were built in the 1980s retained traffic separation even when houses were placed in a grid. It is important to remember that traffic separation was not simply introduced for the benefit of pedestrians – it is extremely expensive and a direct result of a motorism-orientated planning.[222] Lives must be saved. The fact that there is much praise in the literature for these measures is perhaps a little misleading.[223] It is hard to see why forcing people down dark underpasses and across windy pedestrian bridges can be about anything other than giving precedence to cars.

There has been a small paradigm shift when it comes to cars among urban developers in the United States in recent years. Janette Sadik-Khan has noted that,

People want to get around without the burden of owning a car [...]
A car is the most inefficient asset that you have, it sits 95 percent

of the time unused [...] It is pedestrians, not cars, that drive the economy.[224]

Sadik-Khan is also one of the founders of the National Association of City Transportation Officials (NATCO), an organisation that primarily caters to the major American cities San Francisco, Vancouver, Boston, Washington D.C., New York, Seattle and Portland where there is already increased urbanization of the city centres as well as some densification and expanded public transport. Car-dense cities such as Atlanta, Charlotte and San Diego are also realising that they will need to jump on the bandwagon, as it were. At the NACTO conference in 2014, Janette Sadik-Khan emphasized that new and different investments have to be made. "We have to do these investments now, there is no other way to go," she said.

At the same NATCO conference, the Washington State traffic commissioner, Lynn Peterson, explained that attitudes were changing. "We have believed that traffic is an end in itself, so we have destroyed large potential land assets as well as caused a lot of damage to the environment. We need to accept that traffic systems are about land value. That is the purpose of traffic planning." And she went on to say that freeways are almost never constructed in cities anymore because they cost too much to build and maintain.

In the United States, freeways are even being demolished. Some have been converted to city boulevards, others have been decked over. Harbor Drive in Portland was demolished as long ago as in 1974 and replaced with a park along the water. Since then land value has increased by ten per cent every year for the surrounding properties, which is a more rapid increase than for other areas in central Portland. San Francisco's Central Freeway was demolished in 2003 and replaced by Octavia Boulevard. The same year John Norquist, Mayor of Milwaukee and a former activist, made sure that Park East Freeway was demolished and replaced by a boulevard thereby freeing ten acres of land for new development. Such radical restructuring gives rise to new land uses. Moreover, constructing a new boulevard costs less than building a new freeway. In hindsight this all seems rather obvious, but the process was preceded by a lengthy struggle for Norquist.[225] Other well-known examples are Madrid Rio, a former motorway that was converted to a ten-kilometre-long city park in central Madrid, and a long, linear park along the river Cheonggyecheon, which replaces a motorway stretch in central Seoul.[226]

The Big Dig in Boston is one of the largest and most expensive infrastructure projects in the history of the United States. It took fifteen years and cost fifteen billion dollars to bury and cover the Central Artery. The Förbifart Stockholm motorway project,[227] most of which will be underground, will cost at least four, maybe as much as nine billion dollars.[228] The fact that the infrastructure is unsuitable for public transport (for example in case there were to be a radical drop in car traffic) reveals that it is at best a poorly conceived mistake and considering that it surfaces via large ramps and major junctions adjacent to underprivileged city districts makes it positively immoral. Förbifart Stockholm is a 1960s concept, redolent of a time when many believed in a future when everyone would be dependent on cars. It is surprising that Swedish politicians are keen to endorse a project such as this since urban development is now all about proximity, walkability and public transport. Instead of building new motorways, the state and the local council should overhaul the ruined cityscape they inherited and do as they have done on Södergatan in Stockholm, which was decked over in 1985. It is a city-healing project that has caused this part of the city to flourish – Stockholm's very own Big Dig.[229]

Gothenburg is cut through by impenetrable motorway barriers and junctions, but the city council is beginning to remedy the situation. The new road tunnel along the Göta älv, which connects the city centre with the river, even though the park that was laid out on top of it has not quite come to life yet. It will probably happen when a flyover to Frihamnen on Hisingen is built – an avenue leading to Backaplan. In so doing, Gothenburg's main avenue, Kungsportsavenyn, will align across to the suburbs on the island of Hisingen. Healing the city is not just about stopping excessive car use, but bringing public spaces, streets and parks to life and connecting city districts, thereby encouraging social integration.

Freeway demolition in the United States has resulted in a slight reduction in car traffic, but not as much as you might expect. The existing road network can handle a good deal of traffic. The capacity of city boulevards tends to be surprisingly high.[230] Car traffic is a complex system, and it turns out that people adapt their travel patterns to real situations. Car use goes up when new roads are built, a phenomenon known as induced traffic.[231] Traffic researchers agree as a whole that building roads does not eliminate urban congestion. Adding lanes means adding cars, hence queues form quickly.[232] There are of course many examples of roads that have been removed or streets that have been temporarily closed with no observed change in traffic flow.[233] The cars have simply disappeared. This is due to a complex combination of people choosing other means of transport or making minor adjustments to their travel routine. Complex social systems like city traffic can self-organize and adapt. The most efficient way of reducing congestion in a city is to limit parking, introduce congestion charges and extend public transport and cycle infrastructure.[234] Studies made in the United States show higher growth rates in cities with dense traffic.[235] It appears that a city can manage crowding to a degree, but there are limits. I will be returning to how this problem can be solved without constructing new roads. The attractiveness of a city is after all dependent on quality of life, and commuting times are an important factor in this context.

The NACTO publication *Urban Street Design Guide*[236] focuses on street design that takes the city's transport needs into account while recognising the street as a place used by people. The illustrations show how over-dimensioned lanes can be reduced to achieve the right balance between road users, a strategy described by developers as rightsizing. Not only does the guide mention traffic lanes and parking spaces, but also how you can widen pavements to accommodate people and outdoor furniture in small or large public places. Tactical urbanism experiments implemented in New York and San Francisco have been included in a development guide endorsed by America's major traffic departments as well as by the national government body, the United States Department of Transportation. Extensive research has turned something only recently seen as a form of experimental, radical critique against cars into a national standard. The City of New York has made major investments in alternative forms of transportation in the last five years. Fifty kilometres of cycle lanes and nineteen kilometres of new, fast bus lanes have been built.

"And so, I think that the lesson that we have from New York is that it's possible to change your streets quickly, it's not expensive, it can provide immediate benefits, and it can be quite popular. You just need to reimagine your streets. They're hidden in plain sight," *237* says Janette Sadik-Khan in her Ted Talk. A great many books about this urban planning revolution have been published in recent years (*Streetfight*, *Happy City*, *Walkable City*, *Start-Up City*, *Cities for People*). Recurring terms are walkability, livability and placemaking. Professor Jan Gehl, a Danish architect and the author of numerous seminal works about residents and life between the buildings in a city, has perhaps had the greatest impact in this respect.[238] He likes to point out that we have a great deal of information about car traffic at the same time as we know little about how people walk and cycle in the city. City councils are becoming increasingly aware of this situation, and many are now commissioning studies of city life and pedestrian behaviour. The studies Gehl conducted of Copenhagen in the 1960s contributed to the removal of cars and parking spaces as well as the establishment of the pedestrian precinct Strøget. Gehl says that what we need is an architectural revolution. "First life, then space, then buildings – doing it the other way round never works."[239] When we start off with the city life we want, architecture and the cityscape will be very different from the modernist project, says Jan Gehl

The worst idea we've ever had is suburban sprawl

in agreement with Jane Jacobs, Donald Appleyard, William H. Whyte and others.

There is growing curiosity about what it is that makes a city alive, but people are also suspicious of anything that can be described as "citylike". Lars Marcus, former professor of urban development at the Royal Institute of Technology in Stockholm, has in several articles discussed the problems associated with the new form of urbanism that has dominated within the field of urban development over the past thirty years. He points out that the old grid system with its streets, quarters and parks has for various reasons not encouraged the vibrant city life that exists under the surface, which is dependent on, for example, the way street grids are joined together and how that affects segregation; the way parks are designed and where they are located; how boundaries between private and public land work; the way density is concentrated. The buildings are merely fronts, rather like stage sets in areas that are too dispersed, too segregated, too monotonous.

Jeff Speck's book *Walkable City*[240] deals with this problem from an American perspective with an emphasis on car-dependent suburban America.

> The worst idea we've ever had is suburban sprawl [...] By suburban sprawl, I refer to the reorganisation of the landscape and the creation of the landscape around the requirement of automobile use, and that the automobile that was once an instrument of freedom has become a gas-belching, time-wasting and life-threatening prosthetic device that many of us need just to, most Americans, in fact, need, just to live their daily lives.[241]

Speck recounts how he has tried to live sustainably in a house he built himself with solar panels, separated toilets and a German hi-tech wood-burning stove, but none of this beats living in a dense city with few cars, he says.

> All of these innovations together contribute a fraction of what we contribute by living in a walkable neighborhood three blocks from a metro in the heart of a city [...] Changing all your light bulbs to energy-savers saves as much energy in a year as moving to a walkable city does in a week.

Just about every city that is spearheading urban planning – New York, London, Paris, Munich, Amsterdam, Copenhagen and Stockholm – are served by a traffic strategy that puts pedestrians first, followed by cyclists, public transport, goods transport and, finally, private cars. This contemporary spirit among city developers is articulated in the traffic plan for Stockholm, the so-called *Framkomlighetsstrategin* (accessibility strategy) from 2012.

People live in cities so they do not have to travel far to work, school, other people, etc. Travel is about arriving at your destination, not about how to get there. Mobility is not an end in itself. What is most important is accessibility, to reach your destination in the smoothest possible way. In order for traffic to function well and be sustainable, the City will need to change focus from moving vehicles to moving people and goods [...] Cars are important in many respects, but in order for car travel to be efficient in a city, most people will need to choose some other means of transportation. In order for the traffic system in Stockholm to be efficient, and for car traffic to be efficient, we need to drive less. More people will have to walk, cycle and use public transport. Public transport lanes, more cycle lanes, fewer parking spaces and better pedestrian zones will gradually have to be introduced [...] Reducing car traffic does not prevent well-functioning car traffic, goods transports and other commercial vehicles. On the contrary, it is essential. The city is planning for a population increase of 25 per cent up until 2030, all these people will not be able to travel by car in the same degree as they do now. Not working towards reducing car traffic would therefore be against car traffic.[242]

Munich is the car capital of Europe. The city has a traffic policy that is strikingly similar to that of Stockholm when it comes to size and planning traditions.

To create a future-oriented residential area structure through qualified inner-city development – compact, urban, green [...] Opportunities to increase the density of urban development must be exploited in the immediate catchment areas, which benefit from efficient public transit.

The above is an excerpt from the Munich city plan of 2005. Despite the status the automotive industry enjoys as a major employer in the city,[243] pedestrians and cyclists are top priorities and private cars have the lowest priority. Just as in Stockholm, urban planning has focused on building city districts near public transport hubs, which in the United States goes by the name of Transit Oriented Development (TOD). Consequently, ninety per cent of all travel into central Munich is by public transport. Instead of congestion charges, the city has introduced tough parking restrictions in the city centre. Hamburg is another German city where that is turning its attention to urban design. The city council has produced a plan to convert forty per cent of the city into green areas. A network of parks with pedestrian and cycle zones will make the city more attractive. A gigantic over-decking of the A7 motorway is planned. This will add sixty-two acres that can be used for parks and the construction of two thousand new homes.

In 2013, the City of Paris was forced to put an immediate cap on car traffic due to high emissions. Only one in every two cars was admitted based on registration plates. In 2014, the Mayor of Paris, Anne Hidalgo, announced that central Paris will be car-free in the future. It means that non-residents will be banned from driving in central Paris and speed limits will be thirty kilometres an hour throughout the city. The number of cycle lanes will be doubled by 2020. The city has also introduced limitations on the number of parking spaces that may be assigned in neighbourhoods within five hundred metres of a metro station. [244] Five hundred metres is considered walking distance. This is radical compared to other European cities where a common practice is to assign a certain number of parking spaces per dwelling in every neighbourhood block. This turn from a minimum to a maximum norm is something of a paradigm shift.

Travel habits are changing dramatically in Paris. "Sixty per cent of all citizens do not own a car; in 2011, the figure was forty per cent [...] It changes rapidly," according to the Mayor. There are major plans for banning cars along the banks of the

River Seine and turn the roads into parks. This idea was born with the Paris Plage project, when roads along the Seine were closed to car traffic during the summer months. In June 2015, it was decided that seven of Paris's major squares were to be car-free, among them Place de la Bastille, Place d'Italie and Place de la Nation. On September 27, 2015, the city organised a car-free day when large parts of central town were closed to traffic, including the Champs-Elysées.[245] Soon afterwards, it was decided that the Champs-Élysées was to be closed to traffic during one day every month throughout 2016. The Mayor told *L'Express*,

> This is all part of an overall strategy where we very consciously assume that there will be much fewer cars in Paris. So we are not counting on higher traffic flows or a world with more cars than there are today. Objectively speaking, this will not be the case. [246]

She was even more to the point in the forum *20 Minutes* when she said that, "A city in which you are surrounded by chaos and cars is not a real city."[247]

The city of Oslo has been proactive and willing to change their car-dominated inner city and instead invest in pedestrians and bikes. The City is planning to ban car traffic in the city centre, which has been a major topic in the media.[248] The City's new cycle traffic plan was endorsed in September 2015. Over half a billion dollars have been allocated for bicycle lanes over the next ten years. The target is a three-fold increase in cycle zones and twice as many cyclists in the city.[249]

In 2013, Madrid presented their new city plan in which the City proposes to place pedestrians at the top of the traffic hierarchy and ban cars from large parts of the city centre in tough competition with Barcelona's successful bid to increase the number of public spaces and zones, which has turned the city into an international metropolis and a popular tourist destination.[250] Brussels, today one of the most car-dominated cities in Europe, has similar aims. The Mayor of Brussels, Yvan Mayeur, wants to remove cars from the city centre, and a pedestrian street plan has been introduced.[251] In 2015, Milan presented a

A city in which you are surrounded by chaos and cars is not a real city

plan that involved banning cars from the city centre.[252] In June 2015, the City of Dublin presented their plan for removing cars from large sections of the city centre and create new pedestrian precincts.[253] The most famous example is perhaps the way Copenhagen is planning to annually remove between two and three per cent of all parking spaces in the city centre and transform them into pedestrian precincts and public squares. They will also extend the world-famous Strøget shopping area. Just like Times Square in New York, Strøget has become a symbol for Copenhagen, a success story that the city's politicians and are proud to showcase worldwide.

Congestion charges were introduced in London in 2003, and the city has continued to open up more spaces for public transport, pedestrians and cyclists. As of the year 2000, the number of cars in central London has been halved during peak hours and the number of cyclists has trebled.[254] Oxford Street is closed to all traffic except buses and taxis, and there are plans for closing it completely for vehicle traffic in the future.[255] The Stockholm congestion charges are also worth mentioning. Before they were introduced, polls showed that seventy per cent of citizens were against congestion charges. According to recent polls, seventy per cent now feel positively toward them. The Stockholm congestion charges have reduced traffic by about twenty per cent.[256] This reduction can be clearly felt in the city centre, and it has resulted in better traffic flows and more room for buses and bicycles. Congestion charges in cities like Stockholm, London and Singapore (where they were first introduced) have shown that limitations on car traffic results in better accessibility, and that the wider community appreciates the benefits.

The Mayor of Bogotá, Enrique Peñalosa, has established the city's international reputation for building out public transport, pavements and cycle lanes. Three hundred kilometres of cycle lanes have been built since 1998 and parking spaces have been removed from main thoroughfares to widen pavements. Money has been invested in public spaces, schools and libraries as an alternative to motorways that intersect the city. Had they been implemented, these motorways would have increased inequality and lowered the citizens' quality of life. Medellín in Colombia is another city that has attracted a great deal of attention. In 2012 it won the Sustainable Transport Award for its extended bus services, a new cableway over the slums and for having created nearly two kilometres of car-free city space.

Buenos Aires, like Bogotá, Medellín and Curitiba, have developed an extensive public bus system, which has greatly improved the situation for commuters, especially in low-income areas where there was previously no public transport and where few people own cars. By creating separate bus lanes, travel time to the city centre was reduced from fifty-five to eighteen minutes. Buenos Aires too has invested heavily in pedestrian precincts and introduced a speed limit of ten kilometres per hour in the city centre, which is also a no-parking zone. This is not only a radical measure in social terms; it has made the city a safer and more attractive place for investors, thus promoting economic development.[257] Brazil's largest city, São Paulo, recently came up with a radical plan for reducing car traffic and building out the city's public transport system. It includes parking limitations in public transport zones, rather like the maximum norm that has been introduced in Paris.[258] The fourth most densely populated place in the world, Mexico City, is also considered by many to have the worst traffic situation in the world.[259] The city has recently implemented a major investment in cycling. One hundred and fifty kilometres of new cycle lanes have been built and a bicycle sharing system with six thousand bicycles distributed to 444 stations around the city has been introduced. Fifty-five kilometres of city streets are closed one day a week to make space for cyclists and pedestrians.

Attention has been aimed at Helsinki's proposed conversion of all access roads to city boulevards.[260] The motive is to not only improve traffic but also to free up land for the construction of thousands of new homes. The City of Helsinki also wants to develop a transit payment system that includes everything from public transport and taxis to rental bikes and cars. This means that you can search and pay for the entire trip from A to B regardless of means of transport in one single transaction on your mobile phone. You might start off by renting a bike, cycle to the tram and continue your journey by taxi. All by pressing a button on your phone – "The citizens of Helsinki will not be owning cars in the future."[261] Urban designers have begun to look to new traffic players that use smart phones (Uber, Lyft, Car2Go). Digital rental systems are safe and convenient for anyone who uses a car only occasionally and does not want the trouble of owning and maintaining one.

"Today, transportation in many cities requires a car, but new technologies are reshaping the game," according to *Urban Mobility at a Tipping Point,* a report published by the mega consultant McKinsey.[262] "Urban mobility will likely be lower cost, faster and safer and the lines between private and public will be increasingly blurred."[263] What the experts are referring to is mainly the development of self-driving vehicles and how they will transform traffic in the future. Google was first, but now most major car manufacturers are pursuing their own development projects. Self-driving cars are likely to make traffic run more smoothly by communicating with each other and thereby optimising flows, distances and routes. The controversial company Uber has taken over the market in over three hundred cities and is now the world's largest taxi company. Their success is due to a mobile app that connects customers and drivers geographically and simplifies payments. Uber are in the process of developing self-driving vehicles, and the company's managing director believes that their entire fleet will be self-driving by 2030.[264]

One incentive that drives this development is the fact that cars are idle on average ninety-five per cent of the time.[265] This is clearly an inefficient use of resources. "If someone described that model to you and didn't tell you it was cars, you'd say it was ripe for disruption," says the head of General Motors.[266] If all the vehicles in the United States were self-driving, the number of vehicles would fall from 245 million to just under two and a half million – a reduction of up to ninety-nine per cent.[267] A study financed by the OECD recently showed that if self-driving cars replaced all the cars of a medium-sized European city, only a tenth of the current number of vehicles would suffice.[268] According to another estimate, the number of cars in Stockholm would fall by ninety-three per cent and the number of parking spaces by ninety-five per cent if self-driving taxis replaced all private cars. We would have a city without parking spaces and many square kilometres of space would be freed up for parks, pavements, cycle lanes and public transport lanes; traffic capacity would be doubled.[269] Developers of self-driving vehicles agree that they will have to be extremely safe in a pedestrian environment. They argue that the number of accidents will fall radically once the human factor has been removed. There are some difficult, perhaps even impossible issues left to resolve, however. Who is liable when a self-driving car hits a person? How should insurance policies be drawn up? What about legislation? Many opportunities will open up with self-driving cars and car-sharing systems. This will all contribute to revolutionising the way cities are designed.

What will happen to transport workers, taxi drivers, truck drivers, bus drivers and couriers? There are some fourteen million truck drivers in the United States, a much higher figure than for any other profession.[270] Self-driving trucks, for example, would make seven million of them redundant.[271] The automotive industry is clearly looking at some major opportunities, but considering the way urban development has progressed over the past centuries, there may well be cause for concern. Or maybe they realise, like so many others, that a society based on cars must be dismantled and transformed into something that encourages human encounters, well-being and economic development. Many other sectors of business and industry – the growing knowledge and service sectors, and to a large extent real estate – need to learn to operate in a dense city dominated by people, not vehicles.

Business and industry follow suit

It hits me like a flash of lightning. My research colleague, Noah Raford, and I have been walking for hours in Dubai's vast pedestrian precinct and shining shopping malls. We pass big billboards that advertise powerful construction companies with more squares, parks and high-rise buildings, but there are no cars. I have not seen a car for days! "This property market is driven by walkability," I say to Noah, who is the Dubai Futures Foundation COO and an advisor to the UAE Prime Minister's Office. He agrees, but at the same time he reminds me of the city's past. Aerial photographs of Dubai show that this city of over two million people, which was constructed practically from scratch in only twenty years, is completely surrounded by motorways. Its main revenue used to come from petroleum, but the city has now turned to commerce, tourism and real estate. Dubai is the modernist city incarnate. There are striking similarities between Le Corbusier's drawings from the 1920s and the Dubai of today – car-free islands in an ocean of roads. Most interesting of all are the images and environments that are feeding this market. There are of course adverts for high-end cars and villas, but real estate is sold through images of men, and only men, who are walking along palm-lined avenues. Land value is created by attractive, populated meeting places (for men).

The craziest example of Dubai's planning philosophy is perhaps a construction that may turn out to be the largest shopping centre in the world when it is completed – the Mall of the World consists of four and a half million square metres of commercial space. The newly opened Mall of Scandinavia in Stockholm is just over a hundred thousand square metres. The Mall of the World is unfathomably large. It will be designed like a classic city centre with streets, squares and parks, but no cars. Dubai is building a city centre with its own light railway; the cars will be parked in a gigantic underground garage. Some streets will have roofs that open and close according to the weather. The Mall of the World has been called the first climate-controlled city in the world.[272]

> If someone described that model to you and didn't tell you it was cars, you'd say it was ripe for disruption

Environmental sustainability is debatable in this case; the Mall of the World is clearly a project that suits car-dependent Dubai, but it is not cars, parking spaces or roads that feature in the advertising. Instead, people move around in car-free street-scapes that could be London, New York or Stockholm. These are the images that create value. Roads and parking spaces do not sell; they are project expenditure. Arguments like "We offer free parking" or "You can easily drive here" offer no reason for anyone to either visit or invest. If you can sell a pleasant, vibrant place without spending money on roads and parking it is quite simply a better deal. This is something that Swedish and American real estate markets are now beginning to adapt to.

Christopher Leinberger is professor of real estate and urban analysis at George Washington University, USA. He is one of many that have noticed some radical changes in the real estate markets of America's major cities. In his report *Foot Traffic Ahead*,[273] he reveals that cities and city districts that offer more walkability have higher GNP growth and higher real estate values as well as a higher percentage of educated citizens. Leinberger measures walkability by using the Walkscore.com web site. Walkscore uses a point system of 0–100 for individual addresses based on how many destinations such as shops, service stations, schools, parks etc. that can be reached within five minutes (400 metres) by foot. Destinations that can be reached within thirty minutes (2,400 metres) are allocated a lower score. A ninety to one hundred score is described as "walkers' paradise – you do not need a car for everyday tasks", fifty to seventy is "fairly walkable" and zero to twenty-five is "car dependent". Not surprisingly, Walkscore.com has the subheading "Drive less. Live more".

Leinberger has added his own, less detailed categorization that defines 70–100 as walkable urban and below seventy as drivable suburban. According to Leinberger's analyses, the value of office space is on average seventy-five per cent higher in walkable urban environments compared with drivable suburban environments. The reason is undoubtedly greater demand.

"

Drive less. Live more.

"

The market is flashing very large and very loud signals: "Build more walkable urban places." How do you know that? It's because people are willing to pay 80 percent, 100 percent, 200 percent greater on a price per square foot basis for the housing, for the offices, for the retail because that's where the market is and there's not enough product.

Leinberger also points out that not only is this a question of economy, "It's a matter of giving the market what it wants and we're going to get these health and environmental benefits that are just tremendous."

Leinberger also works for the organisation Smart Growth America that has conducted several major studies of urban development in the United States. They are speaking of compact cities as opposed to urban sprawl. According to their latest report, *Measuring Sprawl 2014*, people living in "Compact Connected Metro Areas", which correspond to environments that Leinberger refers to as "walkable urban", represent a positive economic mobility and are more likely to find gainful employment. The analyses show, for example, that with a ten per cent rise in density, a child will be four per cent more likely to transition from low-income earner to high-income earner.[274] It is easier to forge a career in a place where everything is close. In the United States ten per cent higher density means three and a half per cent lower travel costs.[275] In a dense city such as San Francisco, just over twelve per cent of incomes are spent on travel; in Tampa, Florida, the figure is over twenty per cent.[276] UN Habitat has published a compilation of global research based on city type and economy. They have come to the conclusion that productivity is generally lower in urban sprawl because of travel costs and investments in infrastructure.[277]

> The economic costs of moving towards lower densities include increased transportation costs, increased greenhouse gas emissions per capita, and rising obesity rates, in conjunction with decreasing productivity. The costs associated with high-density levels include congestion and high land prices. Ultimately, however, more economic benefits than costs are present in high-density areas, especially in less developed countries.[278]

Build more walkable urban places

Although the price of land in the city periphery is lower, it costs more to run a business there. In 1994, the Bank of America published *Beyond Sprawl*, a report that shows the way sprawl limits opportunities for economic and social development and leads to higher environmental and climate costs.[279]

In 2009, the US mayors' association CEO for Cities commissioned an analysis of ninety thousand sold homes in fifteen American cities. Like Leinberger, they used Walkscore. Unsurprisingly, they found that properties with an above average walkscore were valued higher; these homes were on average up to 34,000 dollars more expensive. This cannot be explained by anything other than a high demand for dense, walkable cities. "The choice, convenience and variety of walkable neighbourhoods are reflected in housing markets and are the product of consumer demand for these attributes."[280] The authors' advice to the US mayors was that they need to realise that this offers an opportunity for them to improve economic growth in their respective cities and ultimately finance the welfare system.

> The nation's urban leaders should pay close attention to walkability as a key measure of urban vitality and as impetus for public policy that will increase overall property values – a key source of individual wealth

and of revenues for cash-strapped governments in a tough economy.[281]

Building cities that encourage closeness without cars seems to be a market opportunity that involves entirely new game rules for the development and planning of cities.

Studies conducted in Stockholm and Copenhagen show that the same is happening here. What can simply be described as walkability is what fuels the real estate and office markets in these cities. In 2011, the Stockholm County Council together with six municipalities conducted a survey of the correlation between the real estate market and city living. There was found to be a ninety per cent correlation between walking distance to shops, restaurants, culture, parks, water and public transport, a coherent street grid for pedestrians and cyclists, and the price of homes. Car access has no bearing at all on the price of flats, and only to a small degree on house prices.[282] One particularly interesting contributing factor is the value of flats in districts with a coherent street grid. This is in complete contradiction to claims that high-income earners only want to live in gated communities. The property market in the Copenhagen region showed a similar result.[283] An analysis of the Stockholm office real-estate market showed that walking distance to regular public transport, shops, restaurants and other offices explain nearly ninety per cent of the difference in office rent.

Stockholm and Oslo are the two fastest growing city regions in Europe.[284] We can assume that the Oslo property market is driven by similar considerations as in Stockholm and Copenhagen. One example is Tjuvholmen, the most recent and most expensive development in central Oslo. This is an extremely segregated upper-class area where per square metre prices begin at twenty-five thousand dollars. This is problematic from a segregation point of view, but it is just as interesting that Tjuvholmen is entirely car-free. As in Dubai, cars are parked in an underground garage.

In 2014, I was invited to speak at the International Downtown Associations' annual conference in Ottawa. The response was typically overwhelming. What I found even more amazing was that North America's most powerful property owners' associations preach the value of walkability and how they increase real estate value through "placemaking". The market transformation that Christoffer Leinberger and the CEO of Cities describe is already underway in American city centres. Dan Lieberman, managing director of Bryant Park Cooperation, speaks animatedly about the way he works with events such as concerts, yoga classes and singles nights at Bryant Park. "Don't hire a fancy landscape architect. Forget great design. It's the people that make places attractive."

"What attracts people most, it would appear, is other people."[285] These are the words of the anthropologist William H. Whyte, who was involved in the transformation of Bryant Park from a space dominated by drug dealers and criminals to a meeting place for all citizens. It is a legacy that property owners around the park have actively honoured and that generates a great deal of money. The fact that the same association is in control of events, cafés as well as park maintenance and security is of course somewhat problematic from a democratic point of view. There is a risk of the park becoming as dull as a shopping mall when commercial forces see fit to get rid of potential disturbances and silence those critical opinions that are essential to society and that adds to its appeal.

Tim Tompkins, managing director of the property owners' association Times Square Alliance, gave an example of this ambivalence in his "Elmo You Don't!" speech. He recounted how people dressed up as Elmo, Spiderman, Batman and other cartoon characters had begun to turn up in the newly developed Times Square. Cartoon characters that agree to be photographed with visitors for money were a common feature around Broadway, but there were reports that scantily clad women as well as these characters were accosting people in the street. Tim Tompkins later revealed that the problem was escalating.[286] In August 2015, the Mayor of New York, Bill de Blasio, and Police Commissioner William J. Bratton jointly claimed that they were considering digging up Times Square and that they planned to remove newly constructed pedestrian areas in order to remedy the problem. It generated a media storm. "There's challenges with hustlers and so forth, but that's no reason to expose pedestrians to the danger that we had before," said Paul Steely White, chairman of the Transportation Alternatives lobby organisation, which was heavily involved in the transformation of the square.[287] "Digging up the pedestrian plaza at Times Square would be a travesty for the city," wrote Project for Public Spaces, another group that took part in the work.[288] "Reopening streets to traffic in Times Square won't help. Congestion pricing would [...] Digging up plazas won't stop hustlers. But smarter policing might," wrote the *New York Times* architecture critic Michael Kimmelman. A headline in *New York Magazine* read, "De Blasio's Proposal to Destroy Pedestrian Times Square Is the Opposite of Progressive".[289] The most radical reaction came from Tim Tompkins. "Sure, let's tear up Broadway! We can't govern, manage or police our public spaces, so we should just tear them up [...] That's not a solution. It's a surrender."[290] The potentially most powerful property owners' association in the world defended public space, not in favour of cars, but of people and street life, although they were not entirely uncritical when it came to anything that might spoil the image of the place; that they could do without.

An environmental scan was presented at the above-mentioned Ottawa conference.[291] It offered several explanations as to why the industry is moving towards denser, more walkable city centres; demography was one of them. The American population is growing younger as well as older. Many millennials are attracted to city life, and the elderly are looking for easy access to services and health care in the city centre. More people are better educated and drawn to knowledge-intensive companies, often centrally situated in major cities. Emerging sharing economies and bartering works better in city centres. Greater environmental awareness gives people who commute by car a guilty conscience and lower status. It is becoming increasingly important for businesses to be located near landmarks and in locations

"
What attracts people most, it would appear, is other people.
"

where there is a lot of activity. "Never in my lifetime have converging trends favored downtowns like they do today."[292] I will later return to the reason why this poses a challenge for social development and gentrification.

It matters that major commercial players, not least in the real estate market, understand that the attractiveness of cities and new developments rely on creating spaces for people, not cars. If the market wants change, this is more likely to happen regardless of what political party is in power. Several major technology companies have come to their senses and are running think tanks that help them understand in which direction society is moving. The BMW Guggenheim Lab was launched in 2011. It is a mobile urban lab run by the urbanist Charles Montgomery, author of the book *Happy City*. Montgomery recounts how the project built rooms for social events in New York, Berlin and Mumbai.[293]

We are looking here at an automobile manufacturer that has teamed up with an art institution. Together they create public spaces with talks, debates, an open-air cinema, art installations, workshops and social clubs. This is not only a trend – a lot is at stake. The automotive industry needs to react to changes in city life. The Audi Urban Future Initiative was launched in 2010. They organize workshops, fund research and development, and award the most innovative urban transport solutions, which is not about more and better cars, but smart infrastructure, interactivity and urban environment. There is legitimate concern among car manufacturers based on the way new technology solutions marginalize motorism. The sharing economy is growing rapidly and is in tune with people who live in the city. Companies like Uber, Spotify and Airbnb offer us access to a service (a car, music, accommodation), thus reducing our need for possessions. Philips Livable Cities, Siemens Green City Index and IBM's Smarter City are similar commercial platforms in which technology firms have a stake that allows them to profit from urbanisation. Business and industry are trying to adapt and look for new opportunities at the same time as the large, old

Never in my lifetime have converging trends favored downtowns like they do today

technology giants are opposing forces. The car and real estate industries and their lobbyists are also very conservative.

Bil Sweden (whose motto reads: Sweden stops without cars) is spearheading the Swedish car lobby.[294] They often like to refer to a major EU survey on travel habits.[295] According to this investigation, cars are the most common means of transport in half of the EU countries; in Sweden the figure is 51 per cent. Where is it the highest? In Cyprus it is eighty-five per cent, in Ireland seventy-three per cent and in Slovenia seventy-one per cent, and these are certainly no tiger economies. Hungary has the lowest figures, thirty-three per cent, and Latvia thirty-eight. Research has shown that there is no longer any direct correlation between car travel, car ownership and economic growth (GNP).[296] This is referred to as "decoupling", that is to say when two variables cease to align. The same has happened with GNP growth and carbon emissions in several major cities, including Stockholm and Copenhagen.[297] To claim that a stronger economy leads to increased car use, like the Stockholm traffic administration does, is not necessarily true. Yet their forecasts are based on the fact that a growing economy results in more people owning cars and that they use them more.[298] Some politicians have finally grasped that driving is no end in itself and that we are facing a future that demands more from our cities in terms of closeness, personal freedom and quality of life.

Politicians who get it

American mayors have recently said things that would make a Swedish politician's jaw drop. "Maybe, in ten years time, no one will own a car.". This statement by the Mayor of Los Angeles made headlines in the United States, not because people thought he had gone mad, but because he had said something interesting. According to Eric Garcetti, self-driving cars, car pools and taxis will render car ownership superfluous in the not-so-distant future. These technologies offer mobility for in-dividuals without the hassle and costs associated with owning material things. Collective solutions such as these would make space available and no more roads would have to be built.[299] Mike Duggan's, the Mayor of Detroit, statement "Freeways cut off and isolate neighbourhoods. We are still trying to recover from that," is somewhat surprising.[300] For the Mayor of Mo-tortown to be so blunt and critical of what once was the very lifeblood of the city is remarkable. It has suddenly become okay to oppose car traffic in the United States.

"People don't object to the density of people. They object to the density of cars,"[301] said the Mayor of Minneapolis, Betsy Hodges, at a major city conference in the United States in 2015. "In Mexico City, our mobility policy focuses on moving people through sustainable mobility, not on moving cars,"[302] said the Mayor of Mexico City, Miguel Ángel Mancera. "We need to build cities for citizens, not for cars,"[303] were the words of the urban development minister of India at the same confe-rence. The Mayor of Paris, Anne Hidalgo, is among the most critical voices in Europe. "We are leading a more global fight against the monopoly held by cars in our city and in our lives," she declared, and more recently, "We want to create a peace-ful city, free from the hegemony of private cars, to give public transit, bicycles, and pedestrians their rightful places. Reducing car traffic will help make Paris more pleasant and more full of life."[304] In New York, politicians are spearheading developme-nts, and, consequently, the former mayor, Michael Bloomberg, stated that, "The streets were there to transport people. They are not for cars ... Cyclists and pedestrians and bus riders are as important, if not, I would argue, more important, than au-tomobile riders."[305] In a survey conducted among American mayors in 2015, seventy per cent expressed that they wanted to improve bicycle zones, even if it meant fewer parking spaces and less convenient car lanes.[306]

There are several reasons for these radical claims, that there are many benefits, for example. "There is no doubt that there is

We need to build cities for citizens, not for cars

Maybe, in ten years time, no one will own a car

a change in preferences, people are going downtown,"[307] according to the Mayor of New Orleans. Cities that are interested in attracting new businesses and residents need to be able to compete with quality of life; studies now show that people are more inclined to pay for central locations where walkability is higher and drivability limited. More citizens and businesses means growth and increased tax revenues that will benefit our welfare systems. But there are also benefits on the expense side. Roads and streets are expensive to build and even more expensive to maintain. The increasing demand on state and local budgets constitutes a major incentive for more cost-effective traffic systems.[308]

Barack Obama and other American Democrats supported by, among others, the American Institute for Architects, the American Planning Association and the environmental organisations Sierra Club, Congress for New Urbanism and UN Habitat have taken a clear stand against sprawl and in favour of smart growth. The strongest opposition against this policy comes from the political right. The ultra-conservative Tea Party movement has called it a "war on sprawl", that is to say on private mobility, the American dream of owning your house and car. In Sweden this is expressed as "the war against suburbia", which is also the title of the author and public debater Per Wirtén's book,[309] an inflammatory appeal in favour of the qualities of suburbia and a critique against a focus on the city centre. In collaboration with leftist density critics such as Moa Tunström, Lars Raattamaa and Johanna Langhorst, Wirtén has published the *Tvärstaden* manifesto[310] in favour of increased sprawl, green areas and more space for children, all in line with the ideals of the urban researcher Joel Kotkin and the Tea Party movement. This appears contradictory, so a more in-depth analysis needs to be made.

In Stockholm, the right-wing coalition has produced a land-use plan entitled *Promenadstaden* (walkable city) to promote city centre densification.

> The dense city is the most attractive type of city we know today. In order to meet the demand, we quite simply must build denser cities […] This urban strategy would not only create safer cities without dark barriers, it will also reduce transit times and create preconditions for more public transport. The role of the car can be important, but it must be on the city's own terms.[311]

These are the words of the former Moderate Party urban planning commissioner Kristina Alvendal, who together with the city commissioner secretary Henrik Nerlund introduced the Promenadstaden concept.

"Build more, not less densely," wrote the Liberal People's party members Lotta Edholm and Madeleine Sjöstedt a few years later.[312]

> It is almost impossible to build well-functioning public transport in urban sprawl, these areas depend on cars, and this is irreversible. The opposite is true in densely developed areas where many people live in close proximity. Density creates preconditions for mixed areas where coffee shops, restaurants, shops, offices and culture exist alongside homes, and this, in turn, reduces the need for transport.

It seems that the opposition against density comes from the right in the United States and from the left in Sweden. Does that mean that the relationship between density–sprawl and

The role of the car can be important, but it must be on the city's own terms

We are leading a more global fight against the monopoly held by cars in our city and in our lives

centre–periphery is coming from completely different ends of the political spectrum in the United States and Sweden? Well, it is not that simple. In his book *Ideologier* (ideologies), Stig-Björn Ljunggren discusses the difference between liberal, conservative and socialist utopias. [313] The liberal utopia is the one that is closest to the city, a melting pot open to differences and new opportunities. It could be said to be close to the ideal situation in terms of density. The Socialist urban utopia is less transparent, according to Ljunggren. The Social Democrats built the Swedish welfare system with its modernist suburbs and housing programmes, these are the type of environments that Wirtén and others are defending. However, as the architect Ola Andersson points out in his book *Vykort från Utopia (Postcards from Utopia),*[314] claiming that they were altogether successful in this aim, either from a social or an aesthetic point of view, is not unproblematic. The housing programmes consisted of both apartment blocks and single-family homes, but leftist debaters are primarily defending the slab houses and tower blocks. The Christian Democrats are on the side of single-family homeowners; it agrees with Stig-Björn Ljunggren's idea of the small city being a conservative utopia.

The Christian Democrat and former Minister of Housing, Stefan Attefall, wrote about this very idea under the headline, "We Must Acknowledge People's Dreams of a Single-family Home".[315] "So, we know that even more people than there are today will want to own a house. It is therefore important that we figure out how increased home ownership can be integrated with the ongoing urbanization," he says.

Attefall referred to a survey, which revealed that six out of ten Swedes want to own their home as an answer to the Liberal People's party's claim in favour of dense cities. His argument is problematic in more ways than one. The above-mentioned study is nation-wide and includes people who live in the city as well as in the countryside, so it is not applicable for urban planning purposes. It asks people what they want, but not what they are prepared to pay for or able to afford. The same survey shows, for example, that sixteen per cent would like to live in a mansion in the countryside. Just like the Tea Party movement, the Christian Democrats are defending a lifestyle. During the political festival in Almedalen I asked Stefan Attefall's state secretary, Ulf Perbo, a former vice president of Bil Sweden, about the Christian Democrats' view on home ownership and driving. Perbo presented one environmental consideration after the other. It was almost surreal. Here was a government representative who appeared to be completely unaware of current urban and environmental research as well as the international discussion on urban sprawl and the problems stemming from car dependence.

Predictably, the xenophobic Sweden Democrat party has officially and categorically refused all urban densification in Stockholm.[316] Being against all forms of change and saying no to new neighbours, regardless of who they are, is logical from an ultra-conservative vantage point. The conflict between density and sprawl can apparently not be attributed simply to the classic opposition between the political right and left, but to the opposition between liberalism and conservatism, that is to say those who accept change and those who do not. One explanation may be that people who accept density are practically always pro-densification, because Swedish cities are normally dispersed. This is very clear from the debate. Those who oppose urban densification come from all political camps. Within the Swedish Green Party, for example, there is a strong conservative line, taken by members that want to preserve all green spaces. Green Party members, environment scholars and nature conservationists that live in urban peripheries are a form of urban counter-urbanists that want to live close to nature. They were having trouble with a decision the Green Party took in summer 2015.

> Denser cities will improve the climate, the streets will come alive and transports will be more efficient. This is a major victory for the Green Party youth organisation and will ensure that the Green Party will in the future be perceived as a modern party when it comes to housing [...] we must also dare to develop green areas and green

wedges. The claim that this would automatically constitute a major threat to the environment is wrong. A spot of grass is not necessarily better from an ecological point of view than a well-planned city district where natural assets are well integrated.

The spokesperson for the Green Party youth organisation, Lorentz Tovatt, takes a clear stand against older party members and supports plans for a denser city. Youth organisations appear in general to have a more positive attitude to dense cities that do not depend on cars, regardless of whether they represent the Green Party or the Moderate Party.[317]

There are within the Moderate Party strong forces critical of urban densification and in favour of the old stone city and garden suburbs. Moderate strongholds such as the villa/small housing districts of Danderyd and Lidingö have the lowest new construction figures in Greater Stockholm. The Centre Party is another strong opponent to infill in sprawl areas. Centre Party members in central Stockholm are, on the other hand, very much in favour of high-rises. There is a strong opposition to densification even within the Left Party. The Left are mostly worried about gentrification, that is to say an upgrade that will increase the market value of property and rents with the risk of affecting low-income earners who will no longer be able afford to stay in the area. Does this mean that the left-wing debater Wirtén and others are conservative? Yes, it does, bearing in mind that they want to keep the suburbs unchanged. However, compared to the Christian Democrats' sprawl policy, they are in favour of density, well-functioning services and public transport.

If we are serious about building sustainable, dense and attractive cities we need to prioritize bicycles, pedestrians and public transport, not cars. As cities expand, more people will have to share the space. This is about everyone having equal right to the city. With less car traffic, large areas will become free for people to use. As noise and emissions fall and road barriers disappear so you can cross the street safely, the city will become more pedestrian-friendly. There will be more space for cycle lanes and cafés along the streets. Parking spaces and over-dimensioned roads can be turned into squares, parks or development land for housing, offices and services. Cars have been such an integral part of urban planning that people have become used to them, but half of all car journeys in densely populated areas are under five kilometres, which means that most people can easily cycle or use public transport instead. We need to plan differently. Cars will, quite simply, have to get out of the way,

wrote Rikard Warlenius of the Left Party.[318] The similarity with the right-wing politician Kristina Alvendal's vision of a city for pedestrians ("The role of the car can be important, but it must be on the city's terms.") is striking. Even so, right-wing parties and Social Democrats have together decided that motorway projects such as the Förbifart Stockholm bypass will go ahead. As I explained above, an increasing number of motorways are counterproductive when it comes to densification projects. The Left and the Green parties have opposed the building of motorways at the same time as they are against urban densification. The Swedish urban planning debate can therefore be said to be somewhat conflicted. There are people critical of densification in (almost) every political camp, but as a new generation of politicians takes the stage, their numbers are dwindling.

It may be a good idea to look beyond our own backyard to put things in proportion. Enrique Peñalosa's policy for Bogotá can be considered utopian and liberal, but certainly not conservative. Peñalosa wants change because he views urban sprawl as a sign of inequality. It reinforces segregation and it stigmatises those who cannot afford a car; as a result, cities are dominated by cars and thereby hostile to children. To Peñalosa, everyone including low-income earners and children, have a right to the city centre as well as the periphery. Because cars are such unequal and dangerous means of transport, cities will need to be dense, green, walkable and served by public transport.

We had to build a city for children and thus for people. Instead of building highways, we restricted car use [...] We invested in high-quality sidewalks, pedestrian streets, parks, bicycle lanes, libraries [...]

High quality sidewalks are the most basic element of a democratic city [...] Each detail in a city should reflect that human beings are equal.[319]

When Peñalosa gave his talk in Almedalen together with the managing director of Skanska, he did not mince words. "We should never ever build urban highways again!"[320] he replied to a question about Förbifart Stockholm. The Skanska director was clearly taken aback.

It is interesting to note that Peñalosa is neither happy with the modernist suburb nor the classic stone city, unlike both neo-modernists such as Rem Koolhaas and Per Wirtén, and the neo-urbanists Andres Duany and Alexander Wolodarski. In Peñalosa's view, the perfect city has not yet been built. He says all cities have their merits, but that there are none that can be used as good examples for the future. "In the future we may build completely new cities," he adds.[321] This is possible since the world's building mass will be doubled within fifty years. Considering that we have completely transformed our cities in the past hundred years, we should be able to do it again now that we have discovered how unequal and unattractive the results were. Peñalosa puts forward a strong argument when he describes the qualities of life a city should deliver, stressing that the ultimate goal of the city is to make people happier. He has partly implemented his vision in Bogotá by introducing a system of pedestrian zones and cycle lanes that link disadvantaged peripheral areas with the city centre, thus enabling people that cannot afford a car to move freely. He has also established a cost-effective Bus Rapid Transport System that has given low-income districts well-functioning public transport. Not only has this led to a more equal city, it has benefited employers and employees alike, since they have now moved closer to each other.[322] The Bogotá example shows that it is not so easy to clearly identify opinions on the political left to right continuum when it comes to urban policy. A policy that favours sprawl and car-dependence does not appear to be the best solution for the future. Not only do several leading politicians today see closeness as the key to the future of cities, so does the UN and the Pope.

The UN and the right to the city

In the dramatic year of 1968, the French philosopher Henri Lefebvre published his book *Right to the City*, one of the most influential books ever written about cities.

> The right to the city is far more than the individual liberty to access urban resources; it is a right to change ourselves by changing the city. It is, moreover, a common rather than an individual right since this transformation inevitably depends upon the exercise of a collective power to reshape the processes of urbanization. The freedom to make and remake our cities and ourselves is, I want to argue, one of the most precious yet most neglected of our human rights.[323]

This is how the geographer David Harvey summarized Lefebvre's book. So the right to the city and city life is not the private desire of individual citizens, but a human right, because that which the city produces is created and shared among us. Lefebvre continues, " The right to the city should not be percieved as a simple right to visit or a return to the old city. It can only be described as a renewed right to city life."[324].

This powerful statement has been endorsed by the UN, as if cities were just that, a human right. UN Habitat has launched a string of campaigns entitled The City We Need; I'm a City Changer; Towards an Equitable, Prosperous and Sustainable City. UN Habitat international conferences such as Habitat 1, 2 and the World Urban Forum have a major impact on the urban debate. The fact that twenty-two thousand experts on urban development from across the world come together under the heading Action for Equity in Cities and Development has a bearing on the discussion on urban development. The World Bank supports UN in their development work. City transport "is about moving people, not vehicles," says Rachel Kyte, special envoy for climate change at the World Bank.[325] The following

the compact city may enhance livelihoods for the urban poor

good pavements are fundamental to a democratic city

statement has been made by the UN Habitat Executive Director Joan Clos, the former mayor of Barcelona.

> Firstly, the compact city may enhance livelihoods for the urban poor through better access to economic opportunities and affordable mobility within the urban environment. Secondly, a compact development pattern may lower degrees of social segregation through closer proximity of affordable housing options to places of work. [326]

A dense city is the most equal form of city because it benefits low-income earners. "The current model of urban sprawl is promoting social exclusion. If you privilege mass transportation needs you are promoting inclusion and equality,"[327] said the former president of Mexico, Felipe Calderón, at a conference organised by the World Bank. The extensive use of cars in urban sprawl is a cause of unreasonable inequality. The UN and UN Habitat are perfectly clear on this point. Joan Clos continues,

> One reason that use of the private vehicle can decline with increased density is that higher densities make investment in urban transport infrastructure more viable. More sustainable modes of public transport such as bus rapid transit systems, light rail and non-motorised transport play an important role in reducing private vehicle dependency. [328]

Clos notes that much urban development is moving in the wrong direction, towards sprawl and car dependence.

> Encouraging compact development is just one strategy for creating more sustainable, liveable cities, but the current trend towards lower densities, combined with urbanisation and climate change, highlights the importance of this approach.[329]

Clos is clear when it comes to how we need to look at urban development in the future. "To provide for expanding city populations and avoid uncontrolled urban expansion and its environmental impacts, urban planners should prioritise densification."[330]

Like many other global urban development players (The World Bank, World Resources Institute, Embarq, Institute for Transportation and Development Policy), UN Habitat strongly emphasizes that dense cities are not only the most equal solution, but also the best solution for dealing with climate change.

"We cannot have these cities with low density, designed for the use of cars [...] We recommend those cities should have more density and more mass transportation,"[331] said Filipe Calderon at the World Urban Forum in Davos in 2015. Together with the climate guru and former Vice President of the United States, Al Gore, Calderon, as head of The Global Commission on the Economy and Climate (GCEC), presented a report entitled *The New Climate Economy*. This report places cities at the centre of how climate change can be tackled. Cities account for seventy per cent of all energy consumption and eighty per cent of the economy. The authors are saying that compact cities are showing the way for how to look at economy and climate change.

> Planning for more compact, better-connected cities with strong mass transit systems will help policy-makers tackle these pressing challenges. Such cities are more productive, socially inclusive, resilient, cleaner, quieter and safer. They also have lower carbon emissions, showing that the goals of economic growth and climate change can work together.[332]

This report also includes Stockholm, where carbon emissions were reduced by thirty-five per cent between 1993 and 2010 at the same time as economic growth increased by forty per cent.[333]

According to the GCEC, uncontrolled sprawl is one of the world's most serious market failures. It costs American society over four hundred billion dollars a year, or two and a half per cent of the country's GNP. Forty-five per cent of these costs are associated with water and sewage, one fifth are costs associated with roads and the rest are costs generated by congestion, accidents and emissions.[334] The GCEC's concrete proposal in Davos was to use the ninety trillion dollars that will be invested in infrastructure worldwide over the next fifteen years to remove private car traffic and make cities virtually car-free.[335] In China alone, the state has spent one trillion dollars on motorways between 2011 and 2015. If these gigantic subsidies were instead spent on public, energy-efficient transport it would result in better economic development and a radical reduction of climate changing emissions.

It is perhaps to be expected that there is a strong connection

We cannot have these cities with low density, designed for the use of cars [...] We recommend those cities should have more density and more mass transportation

between the anti-car lobby and environmental organisations. Environmentalists confirm that the environmental movement has seen radical change over the past decades. The romantic aura that surrounded the counter-urbanization movement of the 1970s – spurred by the achievements of the Centre Party and the emergence of the Green Party that caused some to move away from cities, and, more importantly, the emergence of suburban sprawl – has now faded. The most important environmental organisations are now presenting clear arguments that represent an opposing view. In their We Love Cities project, the World Wildlife Fund (WWF), for example, states that "Car-free and car-restricted areas, public transport, cycling and pedestrian-friendly streets are just some of the better ways to travel that will lead to a healthier environment".[336] In their report *Reinventing the City*, they note that greenhouse gas emissions may be three times as high per person, from transport as well as buildings, in a dispersed area; consequently, the WWF advocates dense cities.

America's largest environmental organisation, the Sierra Club, has an agenda they call Stopping Sprawl. This is how they define the problem.

> Stop sprawl. Poorly planned development threatens our environment, our health, and our quality of life in numerous ways. Sprawl spreads development out over large amounts of land; puts long distances between homes, stores, and job centers; and makes people more and more dependent on driving in their daily lives. Sprawl pollutes our air and water. As reliance on cars and pavement of more and more roads increases, so does smog and pollution from water runoff. Today, more than half all Americans live in areas where the air is unsafe to breathe. Sprawl destroys more than two million acres of parks, farms and open space each year. Sprawl increases traffic on our neighborhood streets and highways. Sprawl lengthens trips and forces us to drive everywhere. The average American driver currently spends the equivalent of 55 eight-hour workdays behind the wheel every year. Sprawl wastes tax money. It pulls economic resources away from existing communities and spreads them out over sparse developments far away from the core. Taxes subsidize millions of dollars worth of new roads, new water

and sewer lines, new schools and increased police and fire protection at the expense of the needs of the core communities. This leads to degradation of our older towns and cities and higher taxes. [337]

They do not mince words when it comes to the "green" move to suburbia. It is also interesting to see that the American counterpart to the Swedish Environmental Protection Agency, the US Environmental Protection Agency, hosts an annual award, the National Award for Smart Growth Achievement,[338] in recognition of city plans and projects that demonstrate the potential of compact, sustainable city living through development. The word "city" is all but absent from the Swedish Environmental Protection Agency web site, where you can find information about everything except cities, in spite of the organisation's name.

The Swedish Society for Nature Conservation has adopted a clear line of reasoning. In their policy they advocate[339] the same dense, compact city that UN Habitat prescribes. "Create closeness not distance. Walk, cycle and use public transport. Combine home and work. Avoid creating more sprawl that increases transport needs." Even though the Society for Nature Conservation emphasizes the natural landscape, anyone can see that this is a policy that can easily clash with the counter-urbanists who are against building on green areas in the city and who would prefer to own homes outside the city. It shows that it is hard to gain support for urban sprawl in contemporary environmental research. In the United States, America's Homeowner Alliance and the Alliance of Automobile Manufacturers actively defend sprawling, car-dependent cities. Corresponding organisations in Sweden are Villaägarna (the Homeowners' Association) and Bil Sweden. They focus on maintaining the status quo instead of promoting change. It is interesting to note, however, that they are adopting an increasingly defensive stance in the debate on cities and traffic. It is not so easy anymore to find something positive to say about private car traffic.

In the summer of 2015, Pope Francis issued his second encyclical, *Laudato si'*.[340] According to the Vatican spokesman no other encyclical has enjoyed such a strong response. *Laudato si'*

> **Stop sprawl. Poorly planned development threatens our environment, our health, and our quality of life in numerous ways**

outlines the threat to our environment, to our cities and that the world needs to act now to stop climate change. The Pope, spiritual leader to over one billion people, is perfectly clear when he addresses urban developers.

> Those who design buildings, neighbourhoods, public spaces and cities, ought to draw on the various disciplines which help us to understand people's thought processes, symbolic language and ways of acting. It is not enough to seek the beauty of design. More precious still is the service we offer to another kind of beauty: people's quality of life, their adaptation to the environment, encounter and mutual assistance.[341]

This is what he has to say to traffic planners.

> The quality of life in cities has much to do with systems of transport, which are often a source of much suffering for those who use them. Many cars, used by one or more people, circulate in cities, causing traffic congestion, raising the level of pollution, and consuming enormous quantities of non-renewable energy. This makes it necessary to build more roads and parking areas which spoil the urban landscape. Many specialists agree on the need to give priority to public transportation.[342]

The encyclical mentions that cities should do what they were intended to do – integrate and bring people closer together.

> It is important that the different parts of a city be well integrated and that those who live there have a sense of the whole, rather than being confined to one neighborhood and failing to see the larger city as space which they share with others [...] How beautiful those cities which overcome paralyzing mistrust, integrate those who are different and make this very integration a new factor of development! How attractive are those cities which, even in their architectural design, are full of spaces which connect, relate and favour the recognition of others! [343]

Many besides the Pope are praising proximity.

The following organisations in the United States and Sweden are actively opposing urban sprawl:

UN Habitat, The World Bank, WHO, Greenpeace, the UN Intergovernmental Panel on Climate Change IPCC, The Vatican, World Resources Institute, ITDP, Embarq, the World Wildlife Fund (WWF), American Farmland Trust, American Planning Association, Community Rights Council, ChangeLab Solutions, the American Public Health Association, The American Society of Landscape Architects, the Association of Metropolitan Planning Organizations, the Conservation Fund, Congress of New Urbanism, National Neighborhood Coalition, The Partnership for Sustainable Communities, The Institute of Transportation Engineers, National Trust for Historic Preservation, National Center for Biking & Walking, National Association of Transportation Officials (NACTO), The National Multi-Housing Council, The National Association of Realtors, the National Oceanic and Atmospheric Administration, the Surface Transportation Policy Project, the Center for Immigration Study, the National Trust for Historic Preservation, the National Association of Development Organizations, Community Research Connections, The U.S. Forest Service, National Wildlife Federation, Natural Resources Defense Council, the Northeast-Midwest Institute, Project for Public Spaces, Smart Growth America, Urban Land Institute, Sierra Club, Smart Growth Network, Walkable and Livable Communities Institute, US Environmental Protection Agency, Trust for Public Land, Sveriges Arkitekter, Naturskyddsföreningen

The following organisations in the United States and Sweden are actively promoting car-dependent urban sprawl:

The Alliance of Automobile Manufacturers, America's Homeowner Alliance, Homeowner association, Demographia, Bil Sweden, Kungliga Automobil Klubben, Motormännens Riksförbund, Villaägarna

WHERE ARE WE GOING?

Trends from four hundred experts

This project began when I asked Noah to outline his dream project. Noah Raford and I were both completing our PhDs at the time, he at MIT in Boston and myself at the Royal Institute of Technology, Stockholm. We were both keen to launch a real research project. We met at a conference in London, and as it turned out, not only were we both interested in urban development, we were also both into house music, which made working together a lot easier. We based our funding application for the project that later became Post Car(d) Urbanism on Noah's draft. This book is part of that project. Our starting point was Noah's newly developed methodology for futures research and my own questions about contemporary urban development and traffic planning, which I had experience from as a consultant urban planner. The premise was simple: What will the urban environment look like in the future?

We divided the project into five stages. Stage one consisted of a trend inventory that was to identify factors that will influence urban environments in the future. During stage two we built three possible future scenarios for Stockholm in 2050, and in stage three we modelled these scenarios in a digital mapping system so we were able to see the geographical distribution. During stage four we had scenario illustrations made in the form of photomontages, which were published in a daily newspaper (*Dagens Nyheter*) and on the Internet so people could vote for them. The final stage is this book. The conclusions drawn from this project are outlined below.

The trend inventory was crowd-sourced via a website to which Swedish experts on traffic and urban development were invited to post trends they believe will have an impact on cities and transit in the future. You have to remember that these are all potential scenarios, not utopias. The experts logged on to a Facebook-type site where they were able to see the contributions of others and post comments. Someone would post a trend, for example "more cycling". It was followed by the trends this particular expert on the one hand believed cause this trend (e.g. rising fuel costs) and on the other hand trends this trend in turn will benefit (better health). This generated linked sets of analysable trends. Some were pointing in the same direction, others were contradictory. With the help of a map we were able to see how they were all connected.

A cluster analysis showed the following main trends for the development of cities in Sweden.

1. More people living in cities
2. More congestion
3. More social networks
4. More Internet traffic
5. More pedestrians
6. More cyclists
7. More public transport
8. More car pooling
9. More goods transports
10. More urban densification
11. More air traffic
12. A more global job market

What we are seeing here are the effects of an ongoing urbanisation process that few believe will slow down. On the contrary, reports and studies show that it is more likely to pick up speed. The UN has forecast that two thirds of the world's population will be living in cities by the year 2050, which means that a new city the size of Stockholm is created somewhere in the world every week.[344] There are both social and economic reasons for this development. Today, cities push economic growth and are responsible for eighty per cent of the world's GNP. The economies of China's mega cities are already on par with that of Germany and France put together.[345] The world's foremost urban economist, Edward Glaeser, has explained how cities foster co-operation, innovation, encounters and competition as well as economic growth and welfare.[346] People find their way to the city to make better lives for themselves. UN Habitat also points out that it is in the cities that the more disadvantaged members of society are most able to improve their situation.

Closeness in a city is achieved through its transport system and public spaces. Our trend analysis clearly shows how urbanization and the demand for short distances require a new type of infrastructure. Congestion will increase as more cars, trucks, buses, cyclists and pedestrians share the streetspace. Densification will result in more local services, trade and culture, but may also lead to a higher concentration of problems such as noise, conflict and crime. Technology will continue to develop. Computers and mobile phones are getting smaller and networks faster. Mechanisation and digitalisation will change the look of the transport industry. Several major automobile manufacturers are already developing self-driving cars. New types of car-sharing systems (Car2Go), flexible car pools (Zip-Car) and taxi systems (Uber, Lyft) are spearheading a revolution in car travel that will eventually make car ownership redundant. The Copenhagen metro is self-driving. Many believe that drones will change the way goods are distributed in cities when mini helicopters begin to deliver Internet orders of anything from prescribed drugs to food to your door. Urbanisation and technology are trends that seem relatively safe to predict.

Not everything is as predictable, however. We are already experiencing the effects of climate change. The question is where we are heading and how it will affect us in terms of access to energy, water and agricultural land? We know that the world's crude oil deposits will soon be depleted, but as new sources and technologies such as fracking and deep-sea drilling as well as new natural gas deposits are exploited, energy continues to be in abundant supply, keeping prices down. And yet it is reasonable to believe that increased urbanisation will require such vast amounts of energy that this situation will not last. On the other hand, it is possible to further develop solar energy, wind power, wave power and nuclear power – the future energy supply is unpredictable.

Economic development – which is in turn determined by geopolitics and energy supply – is uncertain. In an increasingly global, capitalist world, individual cities and states have less power over their own economic development. Unrest in the Middle East in 1979 led to higher oil prices and an energy crisis that affected the entire world economy. Looking at migration patterns and refugee flows in the wake of political crises, war or climate change, we are facing major uncertainties in terms of social development. How will social values adjust when a city's population becomes more diversified? How will this affect new demographic patterns resulting from an aging European population? Will conservative or liberal forces be leading developments in the future? Will we be seeing more integration or more segregation? How will government city policies and local planning be affected?

These uncertainties can be illustrated through a number of potential future scenarios.

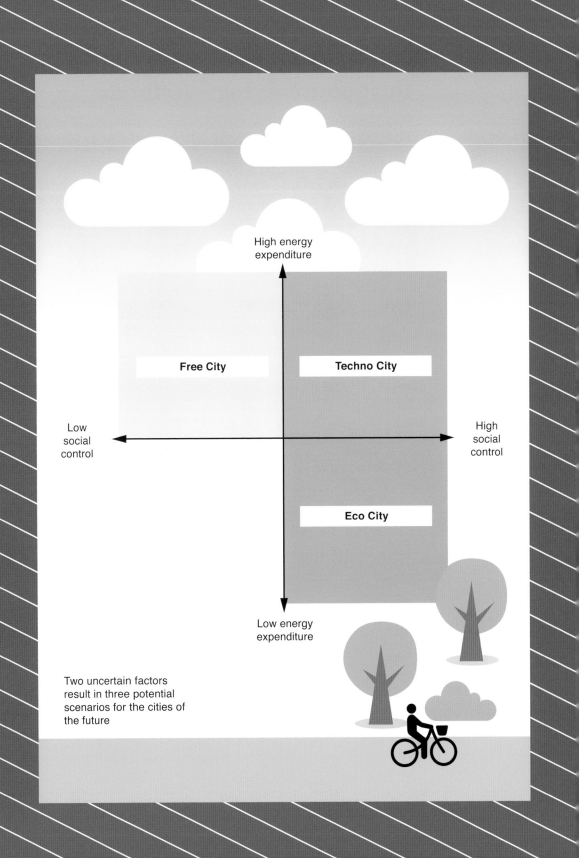

High energy
expenditure

Free City

Techno City

Low
social
control

High
social
control

Eco City

Low energy
expenditure

Two uncertain factors
result in three potential
scenarios for the cities of
the future

Three postcards from the future

A futurist's job is to analyse certainties and uncertainties, and to work out how they can be realistically combined. In our project, we conducted workshops where we explored ways of combining the different trends with various uncertainty variables. How will private car traffic change if the price of fuel goes up? How will a growing economy affect the construction industry? How would a liberal, or a conservative, policy affect public transport? These questions eventually led to three main lines of investigation in the form of three scenarios we believe are plausible outcomes for Swedish cities in 2050.

In order to illustrate these scenarios we asked the architect and illustrator Linda-Sofie Bäckstedt to make postcards from three Stockholm locations in the form of photo collages that show how central Stockholm, an inner city suburb (Årsta) and a small housing community (Bromma) might look in 2050. The collages were published in the national daily Dagens Nyheter under the headline "Postcard from the City of the Future".[347] Some three thousand people took the opportunity to vote for their favourite scenario on the newspaper's web site.[348] Although unsurprising, the result was astonishing considering the way the city looks today. We now have some idea of how potential and desirable futures might look.

Techno City – No Science Fiction

Imagine a future when energy is abundant, a future with new technological solutions for energy generation and consumption that stimulate economic development. Small businesses are flourishing through local innovation clusters and knowledge networks. Income is relatively evenly distributed. This is a Star Trek society where many have access to advanced technology and basic services. But it is also a society where control and automation on all levels is digitised. Sensors and computers used

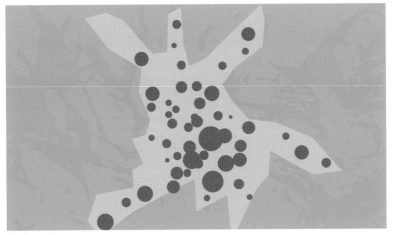

Techno City

Countryside
Polycentric city

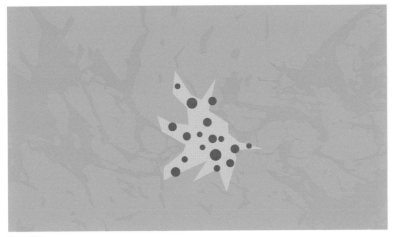

Eco City

Countryside
Compact city

Free City

Countryside
Sprawl
Central Business District

for analysis and optimisation are monitoring all citizens and there is a real risk of social control. New vehicles and energy collectors cause extensive environmental pollution, but serious damage to the environment is avoided through advanced monitoring and technology. This is a high-velocity society where experiences and lifestyles are valued. There is a high degree of social stress since anyone can be a superstar for a day and be forgotten the next. Techno City is governed by a relatively powerful state that co-ordinates urban systems and ensures that they are optimised at all times through a combination of a centralised Social Democrat government, individualistic/hedonistic life styles and local networks.

City centres are denser, and regional centres as well as new, compact small housing communities are emerging around the major cities. The transport system is almost completely automatic with self-driving taxis and rental cars. High-speed trains and frequent air services connect cities. Drones deliver light goods such as food, prescription drugs and toys to your door or rooftop. There are almost no parking spaces as vehicles are now constantly on the move. Technology has allowed more space to be freed and people are spending more time in the street. The dense city environments are better suited to families with children and the elderly, and areas outside the city centre too because of improved services. At the same time, social pressure is higher in the city. Sensors and CCTV register every movement and choice that people make. Life is more comfortable, but also more controlled. There are plenty of opportunities, cultural experiences and recreation. Traffic is safer and cities are more secure, but there is more noise and other disruptions. Cities that already can be said to be heading in the direction of becoming techno cities include Singapore, Tokyo and Seoul.

Eco City – Dense, Green, Car-free

An energy crisis has struck. There is no access to low-cost energy due to climate change and geopolitical conflicts. Technological progress has not slowed down, but new technologies must be adapted to the energy shortage. Micro energy plants, solar cells, wind turbines and hydropower stations are built locally. The energy crisis affects economic development and growth has slowed. The number of small businesses that are able to cope with local solutions is increasing. These are hard times, which means that there is greater need for collaboration and social interaction. Incomes are lower, but there is less inequality. People have to work harder and have less time off. Individualism has to give way to collective values and solutions. Greater state control is needed to manage state-owned land, and as a result protection of agricultural land, forests and natural and cultural values will increase.

The city is undergoing a major transformation. Peripheral small housing areas without access to public transport will disappear due to high transit costs and instead be converted into agricultural land or slums. As fewer people are able to afford a car there is considerable densification at central locations with good public transport and in suburbs close to the city centre; more people cycle and travel by bus. High-rises are too expensive to build. There are few cars, apart from self-driving cars, which allows for wide cycle lanes and public transport lanes for buses and light rail services. Green areas are preserved in places where they benefit city dwellers. Most of them are converted into collective or municipal city gardens. Courtyards and balconies are used for cultivation. If possible, people keep chickens and other small animals. Due to increased transport costs, the city has become more local and more in tune with the surrounding countryside. Life in the city is more environmentally friendly and calmer – a kind of slow city – but at the same time harder and more focused on work and commerce. Cities that closely resemble eco cities include Detroit, Athens and Havana.

Free City – Car City 2.0

Economic growth is strong. Small and large businesses are emerging in an increasingly globalized world. There is an almost unlimited energy supply, and the market is at the centre of this scenario. Greater market control has resulted in a less equal distribution of energy and resources, and not everyone will have access to energy. There is less state control and also less trust in the authorities. In order for people to survive in this competitive future they have to rely more on DIY and local neighbourhood initiatives; individualism and small-scale collective initiatives are thriving. There are greater income gaps, but wealthy citizens will enjoy greater liberty. With better access to energy there is a higher burden on and less interest in protecting the environment and a larger ecological footprint.

There will be densification in the city centre where skyscrapers will grow tall because of high prices on development land. New small housing areas are built in the city's periphery. Suburbs that are today served by the metro system as well as the housing programmes will turn into slums. Public funding for public transport will be cut and tax revenue will instead be spent on car infrastructure. There will be more room for cars everywhere in the city. Space for cycle lanes and pavements will be reduced. New motorways will cut through the city, but wealthy districts with an educated population will be listed and protected from densification. This is a car city scenario where mobility is not solved collectively or shared, but functions on an individual basis. There will be self-driving cars, but not for everyone. This is a city where owning a car is convenient, if you can afford it. Cities that can be described as freedom cities include Atlanta, Nashville and Brisbane.

So what was the result of the online poll? Out of the 3,300 people that participated, 1,481 voted for Techno City, 1,447 for Eco City and 414 for Free City. Four hundred experts within the fields of urban development, real estate and traffic came together at the Citymoves conference in Stockholm where Noah and I presented our results and our scenarios for the future, and we were able to compare them with our initial trend analysis. This time the experts in the room were asked to vote for one of the scenarios by raising their hands. The result was very similar to the result of the online poll. Half of the participants wanted Eco City and the other half Techno City. We could not see anyone who wanted Free City. I was later invited to speak about the scenarios on the *Morgonpasset* radio show. They had posted a poll on their web site, and the listeners were asked to vote for their favourite scenario. Over sixty per cent of the 255 people that participated wanted Eco City, just over thirty per cent Techno city and seven per cent Free City.[349] Although the result may have reflected the young age of the audience, it matched previous polls.

During the course of 2015, I have given a number of talks about our study, and each time I have asked my audience to vote. The result invariably matches the online result. Most want Eco City or Techno City. Hardly anyone chooses Free City – not a single one of seven hundred Norwegian architects, or three hundred urban planners from Helsinki or four hundred participants at a climate conference in Östersund and none of the sixty planners from the Stockholm Transport Administration. One or two out of 150 fourteen-year-olds at Engelsbrektsskolan, a school in the wealthy Östermalm inner city district and of fifteen-year-olds from Värmdö wanted Free City, but the overwhelming majority chose Techno City. At the Transport Administration it was a tie between Eco City and Techno City. The fact that not one single employee at the Traffic Administration was interested in Free City is quite remarkable since it is their job to plan for exactly that very model, including more roads and more cars. I had the opportunity to speak at the NACTO Designing Cities conference in Austin in the autumn of 2015, and none of the one hundred American traffic planners voted for Free City. An overwhelming majority voted for the almost car-free Eco City, maybe because it is so different from the car-dependent cities they have today, a

Low-density suburb, 2015

Low-density suburb, Free City, 2050

Low-density suburb, Techno City, 2050

Low-density suburb, Eco City, 2050

High-density suburb, 2015

High-density suburb, Free City 2050

High-density suburb, Techno City 2050

High-density suburb, Eco City 2050

Town centre, 2015

Town centre, Free City, 2050

Town centre, Techno City, 2050

Town centre, Eco City, 2050

situation many would like to change. Later that autumn I gave a talk in front of three hundred automotive industry professionals.[350] Arguably, this is the industry that benefits most tangibly from a car-dependent society. They first voted by raising their hands and then anonymously via an audience response system with identical results. Only ten per cent chose Free City. A majority, or seventy-five per cent, chose Techno City. It was a result that not only shocked me, but the audience too. A vote at an annual driving instructors' conference in Gothenburg saw the same result.[351] Only ten per cent of those who in the future will teach us to drive safely in our cities want more cars.

There is clearly little support for Free City. Recent surveys conducted in several Swedish cities show the same result.[352] Reactions to these concrete future scenarios are clear: increased car traffic and private driving will lead to an impossible situation. The fact that most people prefer Techno City or Eco City means two things. Firstly, urban development and traffic must be centrally controlled and funded by public means in order to achieve greater equality in terms of quality of life and land value regardless of energy supply and economic growth. Secondly, the car-dependent city must eventually be replaced by a multi-modal traffic system through which city dwellers gain access to many different means of transport that are adapted to each and everyone's needs and have the smallest possible impact on social interaction, city environment and eco systems. Many global, national, regional and local policy documents are looking in this direction, but they are clearly not efficient enough to bring about any real change.

How can we actively influence the future so that cities become a productive combination of Eco City and Techno City and are able to maximise what they do best – bringing people closer together?

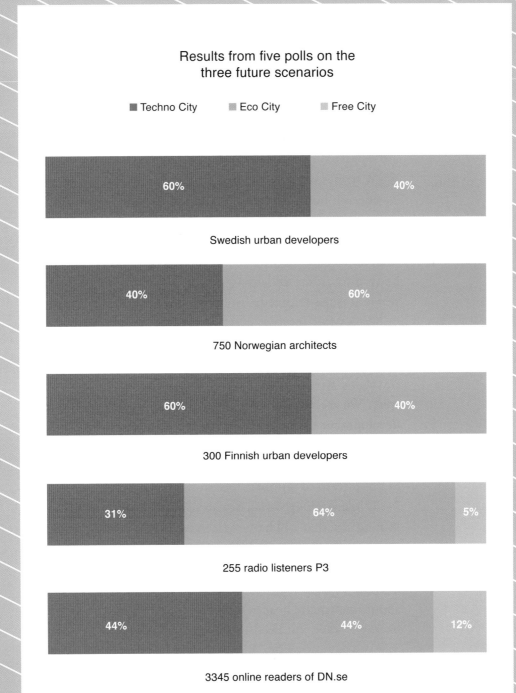

Results from five polls on the
three future scenarios

■ Techno City   ■ Eco City   ■ Free City

| 60% | 40% |

Swedish urban developers

| 40% | 60% |

750 Norwegian architects

| 60% | 40% |

300 Finnish urban developers

| 31% | 64% | 5% |

255 radio listeners P3

| 44% | 44% | 12% |

3345 online readers of DN.se

How to maximise closeness

"What if there was just a ping and I was with you. What if there was a button so children could go to their parents whenever they wanted. It's so boring that it takes so long to go to you. I want a ping." I am sitting in a hotel room, talking to my six-year-old daughter on the phone. I really miss her, but we are separated by a five-hour flight. After we have finished talking it strikes me that she had figured it out! Travelling can be wonderful, but it is often more out of necessity than choice. If there were a "ping", it would take us to wherever we want to go. Erase distance. I turn on the television. They are showing a Star Trek movie, and they have one, the Transporter. It dissolves the body into atoms and transports it to some other destination where it is reassembled. "Beam me up, Scotty!"

When the Internet arrived, people thought that was the ping. If we could just simply send everything by means of ones and zeros and to have videoconferences, we would not have to travel, we would never have to meet for real. How wrong we were. We are now looking at the opposite situation. The rapid development of social media has led to a travelling explosion, from the countryside to the city, between cities and within cities. Internet and urbanisation do not only exist alongside, but also seem to reinforce one another.

While working with a new development plan for Kiruna – a mining city that will have to be moved since mining operations are extending underneath the city centre – I interviewed some young girls about how they saw their lives and the future. Apart from enjoying being near wilderness and nature, they worried about inadequate healthcare, schools and elder care. If you are having a baby you need to travel 120 kilometres to Gällivare. The nearest university is in Luleå, 340 kilometres away. But most fascinating of all was the way they spoke about social media. They were able to follow the lives of friends and celebrities on Facebook or Instagram, all in real time. This flow of temptations constitutes real evidence of their own isolation and lost opportunities. Between 2005 and 2012, eighty-six per cent of Sweden's smaller municipalities lost young citizens between the ages of eighteen and twenty-five to the major cities. This is also a strong trend among those who were born in the 1970s.[353] The futurist Peter Schwartz claims that urbanization is the result of young people being bored with living in the countryside.[354]

The way the Internet stimulates travel makes me think of Taka Sakano. Taka ran a small independent record company in Tokyo. While living in New York he had come into contact with the Stockholm DJ Mad Mats. Mad Mats started a record company called Raw Fusion (which released my first Stockholm Cyclo single). We were a small, international circle of musicians who in the late 1990s got into jazz-inspired house and techno music; we communicated online and played at each other's clubs. I met Taka via e-mail and Skype. When he moved to Tokyo he wanted to promote my music, so he invited me over for a tour of the clubs. I played in Tokyo, Osaka and Ohita, I met a lot of amazing people and I had some of the most overwhelming experiences of my life. Taka later visited Stockholm several times, he signed record contracts with some of my musician friends and a number of Scandinavian house albums were released in Japan. The Internet made all this a lot easier. It allowed us to get to know one another and to play and make music together.

Every other week my children go to stay with their mother who lives a couple of streets away. I sometimes talk to them via video Skype. It works fine, but it does not satisfy our need to see each other. When we speak we want to meet. The Internet has made us more social and more urban. What are they doing, all these people on the bus who are staring down at their phones? They are communicating with others, perhaps they are on their way to meet someone. We are not robots fed on some kind of nutrient solution, we are social beings in need of proximity to survive, to make life worth living – no man is an island, no man is self-sufficient. We all need to meet others. We crave closeness; that is what cities are all about.

I have put together a list of measures that could work towards fixing our cities and maximise closeness. These fifteen suggestions are for the benefit of aware politicians, city developers and citizens.

 1. Turn highways into streets – It is possible to build boulevards that have greater capacity than motorways.[355] Motorways are barriers that consume a lot of land, contribute to lower land value and increase car traffic, so they are not ideal for cities. You cannot make traffic congestion disappear by building more motorways as they induce traffic. More roads generate more traffic, not the other way around. Several major urban motorways have recently been demolished or redeveloped in the United States. In Helsinki, there are already plans for converting all motorways into boulevards. Cars can use motorways, but just as many cars can pass on a central boulevard, and not only that, cyclists and pedestrians can use it too. Boulevards are lined with shops, cafés and seating. They do a better job for all traffic types and add value to city life.

 2. Make every other street a walking speed area – Imagine a street grid where you do not have to share space with cars on every other street, where you can walk, cycle and play. This is what Enrique Peñalosa has done in Bogotá. It does not seriously affect traffic flows, but it opens up for spaces that give, for example, children a natural place in the urban environment. It could be the key to a child-friendly city without large-scale constructions such as the housing programmes that came with inhospitable risk zones, tunnels and traffic slum, even though residents appreciated the car-free zones. This strategy is part of a plan to completely remove all car traffic in cities and to make it harder for private cars to use the streets.

3. Maximise pavements – Pavements are perhaps the most important space in a city. Enrique Peñalosa believes that good pavements are fundamental to a democratic city. Pavements are not just a space that takes you from A to B. Peñalosa wants us to view them as park space. They should be wide enough for people who pass, sit, stand, watch and play. Jane Jacobs talks about "sidewalk ballet". Pavements should also be continuous and not be interrupted when they arrive at a street. On the contrary, the street stops when it hits a pavement. In residential areas where cycle lanes are not necessary, cars can park temporarily on the pavement. It means that unused parking spaces can be used by pedestrians instead of not being used. Motorists can borrow a section of the pavement when it is absolutely necessary.

 4. Build a safe cycle network – People who are strong and brave are already cycling. Cycle City is not built for them. In order to persuade more people to cycle, we need a safe, continuous network of cycle lanes along the streets that attracts people who are less comfortable with cycling. Cycle City works best with separate cycle lanes situated between the street and the pavement, and speed limits for motorists should be low in order for cyclists – both young and old – to feel safe. The world's best cycle cities, Amsterdam and Copenhagen, have safe, generous and seamless cycle networks, and almost everyone cycles – without helmets.

 5. Lower speed limits – The speed limit in Buenos Aires city centre is ten kilometres per hour; Paris is about to reduce it to twenty. The risk of being killed if you are hit is up to seventy per cent if a car is travelling at fifty kilometres per hour, which is the speed limit in Swedish cities and towns. Maximum capacity, that is to say how many cars that can pass per minute on a street, is approximately fifty kilometres per hour. At higher speeds the number of cars that can pass is lower. Even at thirty kilometres per hour a substantial number of cars can pass every hour.[356] To maintain a reasonable quality of life, city speed limits should not exceed thirty kilometres per hour. In residential areas that could serve as walking speed areas (see paragraph 2) the speed limit should be no greater than ten kilometres per hour. In a city where every other street is used for slow traffic, there is room for all modes of transport. Pedestrians, bicycles, skateboards, Segways or whatever transport we will have in the future.

6. Introduce car-free events – These are referred to as "open streets", "summer streets" or "play streets", and they are now found in almost every American city. Streets are closed to vehicle traffic in order to allow city life to take over with events, sports, open air restaurants, seating, flowers, play and games. The streets are turned into meeting places. Open streets should be organised by a local council, but the initiative should be taken by local associations, businesses or private individuals. It should be almost free and permits should be easy to get. Making your city a happier, more pleasant place should be easy.

7. Welcome parklets and food trucks – Only vehicles can be legally parked on a parking space. This legislation must be amended so that anyone can use parking spaces for whatever they want. An online application should suffice, and you should be able to expect a reply from your council within twenty-four hours. If anyone should want to use a parking space for an open-air restaurant, seating area, playground or cultivation it should be a greater priority than parking cars since it increases the value of the public space to a greater degree than a parked car. Try this out in your own city district and see if it works.

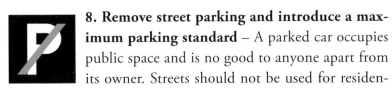 **8. Remove street parking and introduce a maximum parking standard** – A parked car occupies public space and is no good to anyone apart from its owner. Streets should not be used for residential or office parking, car parks should be part of the property you own or rent. That removes the need for regulating parking spaces via the local council and the number of parking spaces serving a property can be determined by the owner. Car owners, no one else, should pay for their parking spaces, no one else. It should be easier not to use your car than to use it. Parking spaces for bicycles should be placed nearest the entrance to flats, offices, shops and cafés. By moving car parks away from the street, they become less intrusive, leaving room for children to play and for shopping. There is a good reason why there are no parking spaces inside shopping centres; they get in the way of commerce. It is the same everywhere in the city centre. Parked cars obstruct life.

 9. Build out all forms of public transport – Investing in greater public transport capacity such as buses, light railways and metros will leave more space for cars, ambulances, fire engines, goods transports and bicycles that require access the limited street space. All main streets and trunk roads should have dedicated lanes for public transport. Buses that drive past car queues are important symbols of democracy. Light railway systems are expensive to build, but have proved to be economically viable, have a high capacity and show the market how accessibility will be solved in the future, thus creating a basis for long-term investments.

 10. Develop autonomous and shared mobility – Owning a car is expensive and complicated. It costs over six hundred dollars a month or about twenty dollars a day to own and drive a car. Add to that the time it takes to clean, repair and service it. People who borrow or rent a car, or who travel by taxi avoid this. It is now possible to rent a car or order a taxi from home via your smartphone. If these vehicles become self-driving, which is far from unrealistic, owning a car will become as obsolete as buying a record album. You get access to exactly the vehicle you need, when you need it. The same goes for goods transport. Self-driving vehicles can deliver goods anytime, day or night, and they make space available on the roads.

11. Expand the congestion charges system – Congestion charges have been successfully introduced in Singapore, London and Stockholm. They have led to better traffic flows, fewer queues and greater accessibility. Traffic was reduced by twenty per cent in central Stockholm, and it remains on that level. Emissions and pollution have also gone down in the city centre. Before congestion charges were introduced, seventy per cent of the citizens were against it, now the same number of people appreciate the system.[357] Congestion charges are one of the most tangible pieces of evidence of the need for central traffic control in order to increase capacity and contribute to the greatest possible degree of closeness.

12. Densify to ensure diversity – Cities have been built densely ever since they began appearing five thousand years ago and up until the early 20th century. Buildings were tightly packed, and cities were compact with a combination of housing and businesses. Expansion exploded during the course of the 20th century as housing areas and workplaces became separated, which has resulted in the car-dependent places they are today. Scientists and developers agree that sprawl needs to be controlled and that growing cities have to become denser through densification, especially in centrally situated private housing areas. Why not introduce a national urban development body through which the state and local councils agree on which centrally situated districts close to public transport should be priority construction areas in order to reduce sprawl, car-dependence and segregation? It is also important that new densification takes different building types into account and that a better mix of housing and workplaces is achieved. More housing should be built where there are only offices today, and more small flats where there are only large flats today. In order to avoid gentrification (people being forced to move as rents go up), it is important that densification is evenly distributed across the city. "It is not how dense you make it, it is how you make it dense," as some developers like to put it.

 13. Maximise active frontages – Cities were built on crossroads where people settled to exchange ideas, goods and services. The easiest way of achieving this was by opening up the shop fronts to the street.

This connection between the street and the premises that line them has disappeared, however, with the arrival of large, inflexible office complexes, shopping centres and car parks. The most vibrant cityscapes are today found on lively streets such as Fifth Avenue in New York, Ginza in Tokyo, Oxford Street in London and Kungsgatan in Stockholm. By placing different types of premises and businesses at street level, the street comes to life. A kilometre-long road stretch lined with shops is preferable to one office tower. These enterprises and activities need the life of the street and they give life to the street. By placing them at street level, they can also branch out into purely residential areas, thus making the city more diverse and alive.

 14. Build new squares and parks – A city without public spaces in the form of parks and squares is no city. The densest, most urban places on the planet have between ten and twenty per cent public space. Squares and parks are rooms for political manifestations, culture, and peace and quiet. Occupy Wall Street and the Elm Protests in Stockholm took place in parks. If you are looking for the most popular tourist attractions, you will find them in car-free public places such as Central Park, Hyde Park or Jardin du Luxembourg. Green spaces brighten up the drabness of everyday life and are needed for children to play in, for adolescents to meet in and for the elderly to enjoy. Research has shown that there is no real contradiction between density and green areas.[358] The densest parts of a city may well be where the best and the biggest parks are. And there is plenty of potential parkland in the suburbs close to the city centre. These include car parks, road verges, buffer zones and golf courses. You need a plan for how to develop parks and squares. This is among the most effective sprawl-preventing measures.

 15. Make child-friendly city centres – It is often taken for granted that cities are no place for children. When people start a family they move out of town to safe small housing communities where they can "let the children out". That is potentially the strongest rationale behind the existence of small housing suburbs wherever we are in the world; it is no wonder, considering the way city centres have looked in the past – dangerous, dirty and unsafe. Inner city parents are reluctant to let their small children out of sight. This was not the case a hundred years ago, when the traffic was less lethal than it is now. If we expect denser cities to bring us all closer together, it is essential that the dense city be child-friendly. Fifty thousand children live in central Stockholm because of the many parks, playgrounds, good schools and pre-schools as well as the limited traffic. But central Stockholm is still far from as child-friendly as it could be, and the space is limited. There are child-friendly, dense districts around the city centre with less car traffic and good playgrounds, but they lack other qualities such as service, commerce and culture. It is hard to find good examples of dense, child-friendly city centres. One thing is clear, however, child-friendly city centres are potentially the best remedy against sprawl. It is up to the developers to convert our existing cityscapes and invest in a new type of city for the future.

Regardless of whether you find this list uncontroversial or too radical, I must emphasize that I agree with Janette Sadik-Khan when she says, "I'm not anti-car [...] I'm pro-choice!"[359] We will have to live with cars in our cities for the foreseeable future, but in order to be able to improve quality of life and welfare, cities will need to be adapted for greater closeness for all. Priority must be given to the most efficient and the most social means of transport such as walking, cycling and public transport.[360] Not least in order to allow full access to vehicles that really need it, for example emergency services, transportation of goods and mobility services. If cars were made for people who have trouble walking, if we saw cars as the wheelchairs they really are, we would perhaps be more prepared to accept their use of space. We happily give up our seat to a disabled person, after all. Car-dependence is really a form of disability, an impediment to a fully functioning life.

A hundred years ago horses were a common means of transportation. Henry Ford allegedly claimed that had he asked people what they really wanted they would have wished for a faster horse. The futurist Dan Hill[361] says that the car of tomorrow will be like the horse of today.[362] When our transport systems have become so effective and automated that no one really needs to own a car, when goods and people are transported in pods that can communicate with each other, making flows and accessibility more efficient, private cars will be obsolete, something a select few can enjoy as a hobby. There will probably be racing tracks and car races, just like we enjoy horseback riding and horse racing today. We might laugh at a *Times* article on the "Great Horse Manure Crisis" of 1894, which predicted that London fifty years later would be covered in a three metres of manure.[363] It was a seemingly insoluble problem for traffic planners at the time, that hundreds of thousands of horses would drop thousands of tons of manure in the streets. Trams and cars saved the city from being covered in manure. Now we have to save it from cars. "If you think we're going to shove two cars in every garage in Mumbai, you're crazy. Unless we figure out a very different urban transportation model, it's not going to work," said Henry Ford's great grandson Bill Ford, executive chairman of Ford Motor Company, in 2015.[364] The automotive industry too seems to realise, or at least it appears to realise, that the car-dependent city is unsustainable and that we need to move on to the next development stage.

There has been a lot of talk about "smart cities", but usually in terms of technology and digital infrastructure, "the internet of things", big data, Wi-Fi, self-driving cars and so on.[365] [366] I would argue that a smart city is a city that literally makes people more social, a city that maximises social interaction and human exchange. That is not all that is needed in order to call something "smart", however. This collaboration, this social interaction must be achieved at no great cost. Individuals, society and the environment should not have to pay a high price. That is why the urban economist Edward Glaeser says that cities are all about closeness and density. People who are sitting in a car on a motorway have not only spent time and money to be there, society has paid dearly for the construction and maintenance of the road. The cost to the environment and climate are high, to say the least. There is zero interaction and exchange between those who sit inside the cars. The humans that sit inside these private car-bubbles in transit between the home-bubble, the work-bubble and the shopping centre-bubble undermine public life and society.[367] If car use were to lead to greater interaction, better quality of life and happier people, it would be worth it in macro-economic terms. But it is not so. Car cities is making people less healthy, poorer, more dangerous, more lonely and on the whole more unhappy.

Reconstructing the city will take time, but we cannot continue to live with the 20th century, car-based city plan we have today. It is no good anymore because it fails to maximise closeness. It has become unfashionable, counterproductive and unequal. There must be change because – everyone needs to be closer!

We all need closeness

How do people in the countryside spend their Friday nights? A friend of mine who grew up on a farm in southern Sweden told me that it is like any other Friday night. People eat crisps, drink soda or beer, eat tacos, watch a movie, update their Facebook accounts and send text messages. People who live in towns and people who live in the country do not lead such different lives, contrary to what is reported in the media. We all need to work, eat, socialize, be cared for and get an education. Everyone has television and access to the Internet where they communicate with friends and colleagues. These days, everyone can see everything all the time. The only difference is that my friend and her family have to drive tens of kilometres to the shops if they need to buy anything or have anything repaired. Our lives are so similar; our basic needs are so similar. The companies that experience the greatest growth in Sweden are found in the service sector, in towns as well as in the countryside. It is not agricultural businesses or forestry that are expanding in the countryside, but service, IT and transport companies. Economist Lina Bjerke has said that the greatest challenge in the countryside is accessibility and a better infrastructure, that is to say closeness.[368]

I participated in a debate about sustainable cities once together with the Social Democratic author and journalist Göran Greider.[369] I guess we were supposed to be on opposing sides of the debate. I was the urbanist and Greider the anti-urbanist. He started off by saying, "Stockholm must become smaller!" Then we began to talk about cars in the city, and as it turned out we were completely in agreement. Car traffic creates major environmental problems and inequalities. Greider later wrote in the *Metro* newspaper that, "the three major Swedish cities could be almost free of cars within the next few decades. This is completely possible".[370] The way we manage to agree about the objective and disagree about the means is rather fascinating. Greider was later asked on Twitter whether he is so against cars

> **I'm not anti-car. I'm pro-choice!**

that he could imagine densification of the centrally situated Stockholm suburb of Årsta in Stockholm where he has a flat. "Look here!" he replied, "Årsta was built in a world without cars. Not necessary there. You're living in the sixties." Göran Greider lives in the province of Dalarna and he is the editor-in-chief of the provincial newspaper *Dala-Demokraten*, but he also owns this flat in Stockholm because he sometimes works there too. He does not want Stockholm to grow, and he does not want Årsta to become denser so more people can live their lives without a car just as he does. My meeting with Greider brought home to me the complexity of this issue, and that the most fundamental principle for a sustainable future is to live where you work.

To live where you work. I imagine that it is the most fundamental principle for a sustainable, equal society. It is a principle of proximity that applies both to the city and to the countryside. Should it be applied in practice, we would be able to cut down all unnecessary travel and reduce infrastructure expenditure. In Sweden, the fact that more than 300,000 people commute to another city can hardly be economically or environmentally viable.[371] Someone told me about an HR manager who lived in a villa on Lidingö and who worked in Kista at the opposite end of greater Stockholm. This person had practically given up going to work because it took so long, and had chosen to work at home, keeping in contact with the employees via e-mail and telephone. Imagine an HR manager who never encounters the staff! I mentioned earlier that the Internet seems to amplify urbanization, but there is also a tendency for people to feel that when they have moved to the city, access to a car or the Internet gives them access to the city at any time, as long as they live close enough.

To live in your own house far from the city and drive to playschool and school, work and the shops every day can never be sustainable, except for the automotive industry and the energy producers. I sometimes encounter environmentalists who are living in eco villages and who claim that since they are living in the countryside, or in a house with a garden, they could be "self-sufficient". Of what, exactly, I ask: groundwater, solar energy or geothermal heating, wood, firewood, vegetables and herbs? But all other food, all other commodities, medicine, clothes, technology (cars especially) come from somewhere else, often from or via a city. We often talk about ecological footprint and that cities need the countryside to survive, but the countryside is equally dependent on the technology and knowhow that is supplied by the city.[372] The countryside that does best is situated near a city,[373] and the fastest growing cities are those with centres of higher education[374] where there is a dissemination of knowledge that makes life easier and that benefits business and industry. Here comes the contradictory bit – without cities, no cars. Industrialism developed in the cities and that was where the car was invented. Industrialization and the depopulation of the countryside is part of the urbanisation process. When technology replaces the workforce in the countryside, people move to the cities. This has been true since cities first appeared, and the process has accelerated over the past century.[375]

"What is a city?" Physicists Geoffrey West and Luis Bettencourt of Santa Fe Institute, California have analysed hundreds of cities in order to discover what general attributes they have in common. The answer is simply that they are places with a lot of social interaction; the larger and denser the city, the more social interaction.[376] Cities exist because they encourage encounters, and encounters generate growth and welfare according to the economist and Nobel laureate Paul Krugman.[377] Edward Glaeser [378] has said that low-income earners move to cities to get a better life, life in the countryside is even harder and there is more poverty. We humans are social creatures, and we need each other while cities offer opportunities. We depend on each other for healthcare, education, commerce, collaboration and much more. The further away from other people I am, the more I risk not being of any use at all to anyone or for anyone else to be useful to me. "Cities are proximity, density, closeness," says Glaeser.[379]

Who needs closeness the most? Who is best served by "spatial capital"? Spatial capital is a term that describes how the physical environment affects the development of social and economic capital in society.[380] Where do we find the most exposed people in society, the unemployed, the beggars, the homeless? Usually in the city centre, near stations, squares and in parks where they are close to others who may help and to contact networks, jobs and money. You need more than economic and social capital to survive in a city, you need spatial capital, access to a location that allows you to live and work, a place that offers added value. This is especially important to those facing the greatest challenges in terms of social exposure or poverty. The further out in the city's periphery you live, the more economic and social capital you need. City development is very much about who gets access and has the right to the best locations, those that provide the best quality closeness. People with the lowest income and education therefore need to live in the best locations.

This is what segregation is all about. Segregation means that groups of people live separate from each other on the basis of class, income or ethnicity, for example in different city districts with different preconditions. The negative effects of spatial segregation are many and crucial to the development of a city. Social contacts and trust are less likely to develop, for example.[381] Segregation leads to an unfair distribution of services, access to care and education.[382 383] It means limited access to jobs and less attractive job markets[384 385] as well as unequal access to transport and a dependence on private cars.[386] Spatial segregation means that there is unequal distribution in terms of proximity to the city centre, and proximity to as many other people as possible.

The reason why the segregation issue is such a tough one is that it partly goes hand-in-hand with gentrification. Gentrification is a double-edged sword, which on the one hand is the result of increased wealth, higher land prices and social mobility, but on the other hand forces people who cannot afford rising property prices and rents are to move away.[387] If gentrification takes over, you risk homogenous city districts and more segregation,[388] while no gentrification of already homogenous city districts may cause stigmatisation of segregation and deterioration of the area.[389] The relationship between segregation and gentrification is therefore highly complex.

Enrique Peñalosa has improved the Bogotá slums through infrastructure and education. In his view, segregation is the result of alienation and isolation.[390] Riots in London, Paris and Husby (Stockholm) are simply the result of segregation. The media reinforce the sense of alienation, but Peñalosa says that politicians and developers fail to acknowledge the real problems and possibilities that do exist in socially exposed, disadvantaged areas. Improving quality of life cannot be a problem in the most exposed areas, says Peñalosa. Reducing segregation is more important than fighting gentrification. "How can improving living conditions, reduced car-dependence and alienation and segregation for the most disadvantaged members of society be a problem?" he asks. This is an argument that reflects the philosopher Henri Lefebvre's ideas about the city as a human right and his critique of the way modernist developers and architects divided the city into functions and human types. Closeness to city life should be a human right, especially to those who are most vulnerable. In cities that experience rapid growth there is today a tendency to push low-income earners out to less attractive areas, further away from the city centre and with greater car dependence as a result. This is a very unfortunate development.

The ongoing urbanisation has led to a housing shortage in our cities. It is hard to see how this situation can be solved – i.e. lack of housing in popular locations – in any other way than by, according to Lefebvre, building more housing near the city, or the city will become less attractive. At the same time, we have to reduce segregation and adhere to John Rawl's Fair Equality of Opportunity principle with a view of always trying to favour those who have the greatest need. The opposite would lead to more inequality.

Many economists now agree that this is a problem the market is unable to solve on its own.[391] They argue that what is needed is some form of price control or subsidy, which exists in one form or another in all countries, including those that are most market-oriented. Regardless of how the housing market is regulated or subsidized, a segregated city costs society more.[392] Since housing shortages and segregation are not only social and economic phenomena, but also concrete, spatial problems, developers will need to figure out how to use their responsibility and influence.[393] Considering the sprawling, segregated, car-dependent city we have inherited from the 20th century modernists, and from a city development point of view, we will need to build in more in central locations. We should make everything the city has to offer closer and more accessible, and also reduce car-dependence and segregation by spreading densification more evenly across the city. Increasing people's proximity to the city and to each other can be done through construction and infrastructure, that is to say through spatial mix and spatial integration.

The former, spatial mix, has been described by Professor Susan Fainstein of Harvard University.[394] She claims that gentrification and segregation could primarily be counteracted through diversity and a mix of housing and office standards, sizes and types. This could mean that multi-storey housing is constructed in small housing areas or terraced houses in housing programmes. Or you could build more bedsits and five-room flats in areas were most flats are three rooms. In Sweden today, we often speak of solving the problem though a mix of tenancies and tenant-owner housing. It makes little difference in new developments, however, since the monthly cost for new tenancies and tenant-owner homes is virtually the same. Completely new developments such as Hammarby sjöstad and Annedal in Stockholm are socially homogenous despite a mix of tenures.

Hans Lind, a professor of real estate, says that there must be "bad housing" on the market in order for there to be low-cost housing, which means that we should be less eager to

> **Cities are all about closeness and density**

renovate properties.[395] Jane Jacobs argues that a city needs old buildings to keep the rents down, while Edward Glaeser argues that as long as the demand is greater than the supply, prices will go up.[396] As an example, Glaeser mentions Greenwich Village, which is in fact where Jane Jacobs lives. The area is today extremely expensive precisely because of its charming, small-scale atmosphere and central Manhattan location. This is exactly what has happened in Stockholm where property prices are rising and queues for rental apartments are growing longer with increasing social segregation as a result. According to an American study, the price of property and segregation between income groups have worsened as cities refer to development plans in order to limit densification, including regulations that ban multi-storey housing in small housing areas. [397] Regulations that prevent density and densification moratoriums also cause inflated prices on housing. As a result, the wealthy become isolated in even more segregated areas, which leads to gentrification.[398] When new wealthy people can no longer find a place to live in areas already occupied by other wealthy people, they create a demand for exploitation that affects surrounding city districts.[399] Old, affordable tenancies have partly slowed down gentrification in some city centres, for example in Stockholm and New York. In others, where the market has met fewer obstacles, gentrification has had a much greater impact. One example is Barcelona's city centre. The attractiveness of the city and its bid to improve parks, streets and squares has led to a greater demand for housing, resulting in higher prices and rents. According to Álex Giménez, an architect and urban researcher at the Barcelona School of Architecture (ETSAB), the only solution is to build more subsidised tenancies.[400] "That is the only way to stop gentrification and allow the citizens of Barcelona to continue living in their city," he says. According to Glaeser and others, the need for subsidised housing falls as more housing is added in attractive locations.

Segregation is also dependent on the location of planned housing and the way it is constructed. Some of the most expensive locations in Barcelona are found in newly built tower blocks situated in vast parklands, not unlike the way the modernists exploited the city in the 1920s. These segregated areas do not fit in to Barcelona's eclectic, mixed neighbourhoods where people who belong to different income brackets live side by side. These extremely exclusive, often gated, park communities are also common in East Asia. In Singapore, for example, wealthy people pay dearly for a view, a private park and a swimming pool. Modernist developments do not automatically have a social agenda, as they did in the early Swedish welfare state, they may in fact be highly commercial.

What makes the modernist city development model problematic, regardless of whether it is built by the state or by commercial companies, is that it takes its starting point in homogenous areas that are separated from the rest of the city. The ten tower blocks in the wealthy Parc de Diagonal-Mar in Barcelona are just as segregated as the 110 slab blocks in the low-income suburb of Husby in Stockholm. I share the Swedish 20th century modernist ideal of building equal, fair housing, the scientific, functionalist approach and the emphasis on parks and public transport. But I do not agree with the homogeneity, standardization, segregation and belief in a society where everyone needs a car. Modernism's failure to create interaction and closeness between people and neighbourhoods has led to a degree of segregation in today's cities that has come at a cost to society. The problem of segregation must be overcome. The most reasonable way to go about it is to diversify construction, to construct new and different types of homes in low-income areas where alienation is growing, and low-cost, simple developments in more attractive parts of town. In order to keep gentrification at bay, it is, however, more efficient to increase density in popular parts of the city, that is to say to build more in attractive areas such as small housing suburbs near the city centre.[401] To achieve this we need control on a national level, regularization and planning.

Another strategy aimed at reducing segregation involves

spatial integration, which means building new infrastructure that connects city districts that are now separated from each other. Lars Marcus and Ann Legeby have in their research[402] shown that transit is more natural in city districts that are joined by streets and public transport, which means they become part of the city. Public spaces within one district are then shared by other districts and daily life becomes integrated in society as a whole. The large-scale housing programmes in central Stockholm or Gothenburg are not perceived as segregated in the same way as the suburbs of Tensta and Angered.

Linking large-scale housing programmes with small housing areas – for example Tensta and Spånga in Stockholm; Holma and Gröndal in Malmö; and Frölunda and Tynnerhed in Gothenburg – with new streets would reduce segregation and prevent gentrification, but it requires a large portion of political courage. Enrique Peñalosa built bus services, pedestrian precincts and cycle lanes between slums and wealthy areas in Bogotá. Public transport is just as important as streets are when it comes to connecting different parts of the city. Peñalosa claims that the streets and buses bring people closer together, resulting in a more equal city. He advocates a humane infrastructure that promotes quality of life and equality instead of spending tax revenue on motorways and car parks. "An advanced city is not a place where the poor travel by car, but a place where the rich travel by public transport."[403]

The price of living in a certain location does not only depend on how much your house or flat costs to buy or rent. Scholars speak of location affordability, that is to say the cost of living and travelling to and from home.[404] It means that if you live in a central location near well-functioning public transport your rent may be high, but if you can make do without a car it means that your monthly cost is just as "low" as that of a place further out that would require a car to serve your everyday needs. The difference in travel cost may amount to as much as fifty to a hundred per cent every month. Time is money, not only to each individual, but also to society as a whole. The so-

> **An advanced city is not a place where the poor travel by car, but a place where the rich travel by public transport.**

cioeconomic consequences may be serious if everybody's travel time increases. If commuting within the County of Stockholm should increase from thirty-four minutes – which it is today – to an hour, it would correspond to another 375 dollars a month that could have been working hours.[405] If you multiply that with the 1.2 million people in gainful employment in the county it would amount to over five billion dollars working hours lost in travel time.

The quality of the infrastructure and the way it promotes closeness to the advantages of the city has a crucial impact on real estate prices and thereby the degree of gentrification and segregation. If public transport is only developed in parts of the city, these areas will be more in demand and the price of property will soar because travel costs will be lower for those who live there. That is why it is important that development of public transport and street grids are evenly distributed across the city so that everyone has equal access to transport. A system of public transport, streets and public spaces that offer the same closeness to all will reduce segregation, gentrification and is quite simply a smarter way of using the taxpayers' money. Governance, regulation and planning are necessary in order to achieve more closeness and access to adequate car-free access in the city for everyone.

I am sitting in a cab just outside Austin, Texas. I had planned to rent a car so I could drive around and investigate *suburbia*, but since there had been a tornado the previous day, I could not get hold of one. The generic suburban landscape rushes past outside the window: office blocks, petrol stations, housing areas, factories and a succession of junctions and road ramps. It is all so typical, and at the same time so generic. It could be any suburb anywhere in America, or Europe for that matter. I am thinking about what had been said at the conference I had just attended, where American planners had praised European cities for their walkability and bicycle-friendly city centres – the way American cities should be looking in the future. I am thinking that this is not true, but that it is great that people have visions

"
If I could choose, I would like to live in a place where I could walk everywhere and where I don't need a car
"

that take people, city life and equality into consideration. The cab driver's name is Cheekah. She is a young Afro-American woman who grew up in Detroit, one of the fastest declining cities in America. We talk about what it is like to live in Austin – currently the fastest growing American city. She is a single mother who lives with her daughter just outside Austin where property prices are lower. She delivers mail and needs to drive a cab to make ends meet. We stop off at a Walmart, because I am curious about what the biggest chain store in the world looks like. She laughs. Inside people are driving mini carts instead of using shopping trolleys to get around inside the gigantic store. We both laugh. Then Cheekah says something that stops me in my tracks. "If I could choose, I would like to live in a place where I could walk everywhere and where I don't need a car." It was almost an epiphany, like in a dream. It was everything in a nutshell, this whole book summed up in one, single life. She had moved from the city in the north where the automotive industry was born – a city that is decaying and has come a long way from its former days of glory – to the fastest growing city in the south where she is forced to live in the periphery and to be dependent on owning a car in order to support herself and her daughter. But she dreams of another life, another city; one where there is greater freedom and where everything is so close that she will not need a car. Much of what is happening right now, everything that I mention in this book, suggests that she is not alone.

My mother has always been an important role model for me. She worked for a long time at the abattoirs association. It was not easy to brag about the fact that my mother worked with slaughter when I was at school. I rarely had time to explain what it was she actually did. She was an animal welfare expert. She established the terms in the meat industry and made sure that animals were allowed fresh air, that their pens were big enough and that the industry did not overdose on antibiotics and other drugs present in the feed. Now that I am an adult I find this inspirational. Where do you need to be if you want to fight for animal rights? Among the farmers, of course. It is from within the organisations and systems that we can bring about change. I often think about that when I meet with a city council or construction company. I am there when major decisions are made; this is where change is taking place, it is possible within the system. We need *external activism* – demonstrations, actions and media debates – to initiate change, but we need *internal activism* in order to change visions and plans, funding, legislation and education. That was how Car City was born. We are now about to change the system all over again. It is hard, but it will feel a lot better afterwards, because what it is all about is the future of our children and bringing everyone closer together.

the city you founded hasn't been built yet
all you have shown me
is a handful of sketches
but there will be many open spaces
the homeless
will be given the terraces with evening sun
elves will get on the bus
and mix with the living and the dead
the traffic will stop
when love steps out into the street
no longer will anyone
jostle with faces
furrowed with opinions and sick thoughts
and so much
needs to be done and managed
everything has not been decided yet
but the nights will be sitting at clear tables
and the city will be all yours
it has the colour of your eyes
your way of walking

"Vid ljusa bord" by Bruno K Öijer (2014)

Notes

1   http://www.boxofficemojo.com/alltime/world/

2   Referencing a major fast food chain.

3   Directed by Stephen Daldry with a screenplay by David Hare.

4   Reader J, Cities, 2005

5   Janette Sadik-Khan

6   Flint, Anthony, 2014, Modern Man: The Life of Le Corbusier, Architect of Tomorrow

7   Le groupe CIAM-France, La Charte d'Athènes, Plon, 1943, 243 p., In-16

8   Le Corbusier, 1929, The City of To-morrow and its Planning

9   Linton, J., 2014, Le Corbusier och Ville radieuse: Att skriva den moderna staden

10   Wright, F L, 1932, The Disappearing City

11   Howard, E, 1902, Garden Cities of To-morrow

12   Hall, P. 2002, Cities of tomorrow

13   Montgomery C, 2013, Happy City

14   Montgomery C, 2013, Happy City

15   Newman, P & Kenworthy, J, 2015, The End of Automobile Dependence: How Cities Are Moving Beyond Car-Based Planning

16   Newman, P & Kenworthy, J, 2015, The End of Automobile Dependence: How Cities Are Moving Beyond Car-Based Planning

17   Key-note speech at the Designing Cities conference 2015, Austin, Texas

18   Lundin, P. 2008, Bilsamhället

19   Lundin, P. 2008, Bilsamhället

20   Lundin, P. 2008, Bilsamhället

21   DN 23/10 2016, Bilplatsbehovet

22   Statens planverk, 1968, Riktlinjer för stadsplanering med hänsyn till trafiksäkerhet: Scaft 68

23   Nordqvist, S., 1961, Tänk på år 2000, radio interview, April, 1961

24   Björklid, P. & Nordström, M. 2009, När kommer barnen in i stadsplaneringen? Miljöforskning, http://miljoforskning.formas.se/sv/Nummer/April-2009/Innehall/Tema-Nar-stader-vaxer/Nar-kommer-barnen-in-i-stadsplaneringen/

25   Lundin, P. 2008, Bilsamhället

26   Asplund, Gahn, Markelius, Paulsson, Sundahl, Åhrén, 1980, Acceptera, (Facs.-ed. /afterword by Anders Åman). Tidens förlag, Stockholm

27   Aretakis, L., 23/2 2016, Paris passage var gatans chica salong, Dagens Nyheter Kultur

28   Peter Gabriel, 1986

29   Ham et al, 2005, Trends in Walking for Transportation in the United States, 1995 and 2001, Preventive Chronic Disease 4, no. 2

30   Cramer, M, 2006, Fahrradnutzung in Europa

31   LSE Cities, 2014, Stockholm: Green Economy Leader Report

32   Mikael Colville-Andersen, Twitter handle @copenhagenize, has also produced the Copenhagenize Index, which ranks cities in terms of how bicycle-friendly they are. I wonder how the citizens of Amsterdam like to be ranked after Copenhagen in the Copenhagenize Index? Would an Amsterdamize Index be a viable solution?

33   Rode, P et al, 2014, Accessibility in Cities: Transport and Urban Form, NCE Cities – Paper 03, LSE Cities

34   Dunphy K. & Fisher R., 1996, Congestion, and Density: New Insights. Transportation Research Record, 1552, 89-96

35   Ewing R. & Cervero R., 2010, Travel and The

Built Environment: A Meta Analysis, J. Am.
Plan. Assoc., 76 (3)

36 The Global Commission on the Economy and
Climate, 2014, The New Climate Economy

37 UN Habitat, 2012, Urban Planning for City
Leaders

38 Holmberg, B. & Brundell-Freij, K., 2012,
Bebyggelsestruktur, resande och energi för
persontransporter

39 Tornberg, P., & Eriksson, I-M., 2012,
Stadsstruktur och transportrelaterad klimat-
påverkan: En kunskapsöversikt

40 LSE, 2013, Stockholm Green Economy Leader
Report

41 Rode, P et al, 2014, Accessibility in Cities:
Transport and Urban Form, NCE Cities –
Paper 03, LSE Cities

42 UN Habitat, 2012, Urban Planning for City
Leaders

43 Rode, P et al, 2014, Accessibility in Cities:
Transport and Urban Form, NCE Cities –
Paper 03, LSE Cities

44 Litman, T, 2015, Analysis of Public Policies
that Unintentionally Encourage and Subsidize
Urban Sprawl, NCE Cities – Sprawl Subsidy
Report, Victoria Transport Policy Institute,
LSE Cities

45 TRF, 2007, Befolkning, sysselsättning och
ekonomisk utveckling i Östra Mellansverige:
framskrivning för år 2050, Arbetsmaterial
5:2007

46 Litman, T, 2015, Analysis of Public Policies
that Unintentionally Encourage and Subsidize
Urban Sprawl, NCE Cities – Sprawl Subsidy
Report, Victoria Transport Policy Institute,
LSE Cities

47 Rode, P et al, 2014, Accessibility in Cities:
Transport and Urban Form, NCE Cities –
Paper 03, LSE Cities

48 Laidley, 2015, Measuring Sprawl: A New
Index, Recent Trends, and Future Research

49 IPCC, 2015, Climate Change 2014: Mitiga-
tion of Climate Change

50 Wikipedia, 2015, https://en.wikipedia.org/
wiki/Urban_heat_island

51 Smart Growth America & New Jersey Future,
2015, Roads in New Jersey

52 Litman, T, 2015, Analysis of Public Policies
that Unintentionally Encourage and Subsidize
Urban Sprawl, NCE Cities – Sprawl Subsidy
Report, Victoria Transport Policy Institute,
LSE Cities

53 World Resources Institute, 2015, Cities Safer
By Design

54 Dumbaugh, E., and R. Rae. 2009. Safe Urban
Form: Revisiting the Relationship Between
Community Design and Traffic Safety. Journal
of the American Planning Association 75 (3):
309–329.

55 Florida, R. 2015, The Geography of Car
Deaths in America, Citylab, http://www.
citylab.com/commute/2015/10/the-geography-
of-car-deaths-in-america/410494/

56 UN Habitat, 2015, A New Strategy of Sustainable Neighbourhood Planning: Five principles
- Urban Planning Discussion Note 3

57 Litman, T, 2015, Analysis of Public Policies
that Unintentionally Encourage and Subsidize
Urban Sprawl, NCE Cities – Sprawl Subsidy
Report, Victoria Transport Policy Institute,
LSE Cities

58 Sustainable prosperity, 2013, Suburban Sprawl:

Exposing Hidden Costs, Identifying Innovations

59   CDOT, 2012, Effect of Connectivity on Fire Station Service Area & Capital Facilities Planning: Looking at Connectivity from an Emergency Response Perspective, Charlotte Department of Transportation; presentation at www.charlotteobserver.com/static/images/pdf/CNUPresentation.pdf.

60   Krugman, P, 28/7 2013, Stranded by Sprawl, New York Times

61   http://movingforward.discoursemedia.org/costofcommute/

62   Gössling, S. & Choi, A. S., 2015, Transport Transitions in Copenhagen: Comparing the Cost of Cars and Bicycles, Ecological Economics, Vol 113

63   Sadik-Khan, J. & Solomonow, S, 2016, Streetfight: Handbook for an Urban Revolution

64   Rode, P et al, 2014, Accessibility in Cities: Transport and Urban Form, NCE Cities – Paper 03, LSE Cities

65   Skärgården magazine, October, 2014

66   Biderman, C., 2008, São Paulo's Urban Transport Infrastructure, LSE Cities, https://lsecities.net/media/objects/articles/sao-paulo-urban-transport-infrastructure/en-gb/

67   Næss, P, 2009, The Challenge of Sustainable Mobility and Development in Urban Planning and Development in Oslo Metropolitan Area, TOI report 1024/2009

68   Börjesson, M., Jonsson, R. D., Lundberg, M., 2012, The Long Term Social Benefits of Transit. A Case Study of the Stockholm Metro. Transportation Research Board 91st Annual Meeting, Washington D.C.

69   Cox, W, 2006, War on the Dream: How Anti-Sprawl Policy Threatens the Quality of Life

70   Joel Kotkin, Wall Street Journal, 6/8 2013

71   Joel Kotkin, Forbes, 8/8 2013

72   Glaeser, E, 2011, Triumph of the City: How Our Greatest Invention Makes Us Richer, Smarter, Greener, Healthier, and Happier

73   Regionala miljödagen, 14 april 2015, Aula Medica, Karolinska Institutet

74   Treijs, E, 19/5 2013, Sara Danius: "Flyttarna gjorde mig till ett slags sociolog", SvD Kultur, http://www.svd.se/sara-danius-flyttarna-gjorde-mig-till-ett-slags-sociolog

75   TEMO, 2001, Så upplever stockholmarna sin stad: Med perspektiv på hållbar utveckling i stadsdelarna, Medborgarenkät 2001, Miljöförvaltningen

76   USK, 2004, Stadsdelsinvånarna om miljö och miljövanor i Stockholm 2004: Medborgarenkät 2004, by Jan-Ivar Ivarsson for Miljöförvaltningen, Stockholm

77   Ståhle, A. 2010, "More Green Space in a Denser City: Critical Relations Between User Experience and Urban Form", URBAN DESIGN International (2010) 15, 47–67.

78   Jacobs, J., 1961, The Death and Life of Great American Cities

79   Newman, p. & Kenworthy, J., 2015, The End of Automobile Dependence: How Cities are Moving Beyond Car-based Planning

80   Gullberg, A. 2015, Här finns den lediga kapaciteten i storstadstrafiken, KTH Centre for Sustainable Communications

81   Lewis Mumford, https://en.wikiquote.org/wiki/Talk:Lewis_Mumford

82   Mann, A., 17/6 2014, What's Up With

That: Building Bigger Roads Actually Makes Traffic Worse, Wired, http://www.wired.com/2014/06/wuwt-traffic-induced-demand/

83   Trafikanalys, 2015, Peak car i sikte? PM 2015:14

84   Newman, P & Kenworthy, J, 2015, The End of Automobile Dependence: How Cities are Moving Beyond Car-based Planning

85   Newman, P & Kenworthy, J, 2015, The End of Automobile Dependence: How Cities are Moving Beyond Car-based Planning

86   Eriksson, E, 2/4 2013, Le Corbusiers framtid har blivit historia, SvD Under strecket, http://www.svd.se/le-corbusiers-framtid-har-blivit-historia

87   Samuel, Henry, 16/4 2015, Le Corbusier was 'Militant Fascist', Two New Books on French Architect Claim, The Telegraph http://www.telegraph.co.uk/news/worldnews/europe/france/11543431/Le-Corbusier-was-militant-fascist-two-new-books-on-French-architect-claim.html

88   Kåreland, L, 28/6 2015, Omöjligt att blunda för Le Corbusiers fascism, SvD Under strecket, http://www.svd.se/omojligt-att-blunda-for-le-corbusiers-fascism

89   Appleyard, D., 1981 Livable Streets

90   https://www.ted.com/talks/enrique_penalosa_why_buses_represent_democracy_in_action

91   Montgomery, C., 2013, Happy City

92   Gullberg, A. 2015, Här finns den lediga kapaciteten i storstadstrafiken, KTH Centre for Sustainable Communications

93   Stromberg, J, 2014, Manhattan Would Need 48 New Bridges if Everyone Drove. Here's What it Would Look Like, Vox Life, http://www.vox.com/2014/12/10/7372787/manhattan-bridges

94   International Energy Agency, 2015, Transport, http://www.iea.org/aboutus/faqs/transport/

95   SCB, 2015, Fordonsstatistik, http://www.scb.se/tk1001/

96   Better Institutions, 2016, Mapped: All 200 Square Miles of Parking in LA County, as One Giant Parking Lot, http://www.betterinstitutions.com/blog/2016/1/2/map-a-parking-lot-with-all-of-la-countys-186-million-parking-spaces

97   Jaffe, E., 2015, How Parking Conquered L.A., Citylab, http://www.citylab.com/commute/2015/12/parking-los-angeles-maps-study/418593/

98   Chester et al, 2010, Parking Infrastructure: Energy, Emissions, and Automobile Life-cycle Environmental Accounting, Environmental Research Letters, Volume 5, Number 3

99   Litman, T, 2015, Analysis of Public Policies That Unintentionally Encourage and Subsidize Urban Sprawl, NCE Cities – Sprawl Subsidy Report, Victoria Transport Policy Institute, LSE Cities

100   Gullberg et al. 2007, Stockholmsparkering: Mellan allas nytta och individuellt förtret, Stockholmiana

101   Calculations made by the architect Sara CW Johansson from the organisation Happy Sweden.

102   Planka.Nu, 2011, Trafikmaktordningen

103   City of Copenhagen, 2014, Good, Better, Fast: The City of Copenhagen's Bicycle Strategy 2011–2025

104   Reid, C, 2015, Roads Were Not Built for Cars:

How Cyclists Were the First to Push for Good Roads and Became the Pioneers of Motoring (preface by the chairman of the British Automobile Association)

105 Cycling Embassy of Denmark, http://www.cycling-embassy.dk/

106 People for bikes, 2015, Green lane project, http://www.peopleforbikes.org/green-lane-project/pages/protected-bike-lanes-101

107 Fried, B., 2008, Study Confirms: Safer Bike Routes Get More People Riding, Streetsblog NYC, http://www.streetsblog.org/2008/10/20/study-confirms-safer-bike-routes-get-more-people-riding/

108 Oslo kommune, 2014, Oslo sykkelstrategi 2015–2025

109 Stockholms stad, 2012, Stockholms cykelplan

110 Stockholms stad, 2012, Stockholms cykelplan

111 Almqvist, E. E., 1/3 2015, Världens cyklister tvingas bli aktivister, SvD Kultur, http://www.svd.se/varldens-cyklister-tvingas-bli-aktivister

112 Spacescape, 2012, Analys av Stockholm City

113 These data were also published in a major article in Dagens Nyheter Stockholm, on May 26, 2012, in connection with an interview with the author.

114 Conversation with traffic planner Daniel Firth, 2015

115 E-mail from a traffic planner in New York City, 2015

116 Rudberg, E. (ed.), 2004, Tage William-Olsson stridbar planerare och visionär arkitekt

117 Sadik-Khan, J & Solomonow, S, 2016, Streetfight: Handbook for an urban revolution

118 Stockholms stad, 2011, Slussens stadsliv nu och sen

119 Hellekant, J., 26/11 2011, Nu tar kulturprofiler strid för Slussen, SvD Kultur, http://www.svd.se/nu-tar-kulturprofiler-strid-for-slussen

120 Alton, P., 28/11 2011, Kulturslussen – ett elegantare och känsligare förslag, DN Kultur, http://www.dn.se/kultur-noje/kulturdebatt/peder-alton-kulturslussen-ett-elegantare-och-kansligare-forslag/

121 Bil Sweden, 2015, Fordon i samhället, http://www.bilsweden.se/fordon-i-samhallet

122 Sustainable Prosperuty, 2015, The Cost of Sprawl, http://thecostofsprawl.com/

123 Skatteverket, 2015, Avdrag – Resor till och från arbetet, https://www.skatteverket.se/privat/sjalvservice/svarpavanligafragor/avdrag/privatarbetsresorfaq/jagkorbiltillmittarbetevilketavdragkanjagfa.5.10010ec103545f243e80001517.html

124 Tottmar, M, 28/6 2011, Höjd p-avgift ska få bort bilarna, DN Ekonomi, http://www.dn.se/ekonomi/hojd-p-avgift-ska-fa-bort-bilarna/

125 Lundin, P. 2014, Bilsamhället

126 Jordan, J., 26/12 2012, The Death of the American Shopping Mall, Citylab, http://www.citylab.com/work/2012/12/death-american-shopping-mall/4252/

127 Fortune, 2015, Global 500, http://fortune.com/global500/

128 Bengtsson, E-M., 21/11 2006, Köpcentrum tar över handeln, DN Ekonomi, http://www.dn.se/ekonomi/kopcentrum-tar-over-handeln/

129 Tottmar, M, 21/2/2016, Flykten från förorten – Hamnar i ingenmansland, Dagens Nyheter Sthlm

130 Montgomery C. 2013, Happy City

131 Auto Alliance, 2015, Auto Jobs & Economics,

http://www.autoalliance.org/auto-jobs-and-economics/quick-facts

132 Bil Sweden, 2015, Utan bilen stannar Sverige: Jobb & tillväxt, http://www.utanbilenstannarsverige.se/jobb-tillvaxt

133 Fortune, 2015, Global 500, http://fortune.com/global500/

134 Trafikverket, 2012, E4 Förbifart Stockholm, VST_001

135 Regionplanekontoret et al, 2012, Värdering av stadskvaliteter

136 Wikipedia, 2015, http://en.wikipedia.org/wiki/Induced_demand

137 Newman, P & Kenworthy, J, 2015, The End of Automobile Dependence: How Cities are Moving Beyond Car-based Planning

138 Jaffe, E., 11/11 2015, California's DOT Admits That More Roads Mean More Traffic, Citylab, http://www.citylab.com/commute/2015/11/californias-dot-admits-that-more-roads-mean-more-traffic/415245/

139 Mann, A., 17/6 2014, What's Up With That: Building Bigger Roads Actually Makes Traffic Worse, Wired, http://www.wired.com/2014/06/wuwt-traffic-induced-demand/

140 Gustafsson, A., 19/12 2015, Norra länken gav mer biltrafik, DN Sthlm, http://www.dn.se/arkiv/dn-stockholm/norra-lanken-gav-mer-biltrafik

141 Habermas, J 1981, The Theory of Communicative Action, vol. 2, Lifeworld and System: A Critique of Functionalist Reason

142 Seinfeld, J, 1994, Seinlanguage

143 Hagman, O. 2002, Fordon och samhälle

144 Schiller, P L. et al, 2012, An Introduction to Sustainable Transportation

145 Cederlund H-Å & Lewin C, 2005, Män och kvinnor i trafiken, VTI rapport 522

146 Gustavsson, A., 14/12 2015, Väx upp från era barnsliga asfaltsdrömmar, ETC, http://www.etc.se/ledare/vax-upp-fran-era-barnsliga-asfaltsdrommar

147 Auchincloss, A. 2014. Public Parking Fees and Fines, Public Works Management & Policy

148 Lobo, R., 31/7 2014, Study: Rio de Janeiro and São Paulo Lost USD 43 Billion From Traffic Congestion in 2013, The CityFix, http://thecityfix.com/blog/study-rio-de-janeiro-sao-paulo-brazil-43-billion-traffic-congestion-2013-car-commuters-renato-lobo/

149 Squatriglia, C., 14/12 2010, These Are America's Worst, Best Commutes, Wired, http://www.wired.com/2010/12/these-are-americas-worst-best-commutes/

150 Delucchi, M A, 2000, Environmental Externalities of Motor-vehicle Use in the US, Journal of Transport Economics and Policy, Vol 34, Part 2

151 Stokes, T., 17/8 2012, Urban Land Set to Triple By 2030, Study Suggests, LiveScience, http://www.livescience.com/23254-global-urban-expasion-map.html

152 VTI, 2006, Biotopfragmentering till följd av transportinfrastrukturen. COST 341 svensk nationell kunskapsöversikt

153 Forman et al, 2002, Road Ecology: Science and Solutions

154 Milesi et al, 2005, A Strategy for Mapping and Modelling the Ecological Effects of US Lawns

155 Forman, R T T & Alexander L E, 1998, Roads and Their Major Ecological Effects

156 Appleyard, D. 1981, Livable Streets

157 World Resources Institute, 2015, Cities Safer

by Design

158 WHO, 2007, Youth and Road Safety

159 Montenegro, R., 2015, Los Angeles, Automobile Mecca, Doubles Down on Bus and Bicycle Infrastructure, Big think, http://bigthink.com/ideafeed/los-angeles-doubles-down-on-bus-and-bicycle-infrastructure

160 BBC News, 28/12 2015, Italy Smog: Milan and Rome Ban Cars as Pollution Rises, http://www.bbc.com/news/world-europe-35188685

161 BBC News, 1/1 2016, Delhi Begins Car Rationing to Curb Pollution, http://www.bbc.co.uk/news/world-asia-india-35203837

162 NBC News, 7/12 2015, Beijing Issues 1st Smog Red Alert, Orders Half of Cars Off Roads, http://www.nbcnews.com/news/china/beijing-issues-1st-smog-red-alert-orders-half-cars-roads-n475351

163 Pak, J., 15/12 2015, Chinese Buy up Bottles of Fresh Air From Canada, The Telegraph, http://www.telegraph.co.uk/news/worldnews/asia/china/12051354/Chinese-buy-up-bottles-of-fresh-air-from-Canada.html

164 Pak, J., 15/12 2015, Chinese Buy up Bottles of Fresh Air From Canada, The Telegraph,

165 Montgomery, C. 2013, Happy City

166 Lund, L., 4/8 2015, Ny forskning: Avgaser kopplas till demens, DN, http://www.dn.se/nyheter/vetenskap/ny-forskning-avgaser-kopplas-till-demens/

167 Regionplanekontoret, 2012, Värdering av stadskvaliteter

168 Halperin, H. 2014, Environmental Noise and Sleep Disturbances: A Threat to Health? Sleep Science, Volume 7, Issue 4, December 2014, Pages 209–212

169 Glaeser, E, 2011, Triumph of the City

170 Montgomery, C. 2013, Happy City

171 Frank L, Devlin A, Johnstone S & van Loon J, 2010, Neighbourhood Design, Travel, and Health in Metro Vancouver: Using a Walkability Index

172 Eriksson, U., 2013, Neighborhood Environment and Physical Activity

173 http://ki.se/forskning/fa-upp-pulsen-30-minuter-per-dag, se även Wahlberg, P., 2015, PXP: Ditt bästa jag

174 New Climate Economy, 2015, http://newclimateeconomy.net/

175 Zhang, T. 2005, Product Ecological Footprint: Environmental Analysis of the Generic American Automobile

176 Russel, K., Gates, G., Keller, J., Watkins, W., 5/1 2016, How Volkswagen Got Away With Diesel Deception, The New York Times, http://www.nytimes.com/interactive/2015/09/22/business/international/vw-volkswagen-emissions-explainer.html?_r=0

177 http://www.volvocars.com/intl/about/our-innovation-brands/intellisafe/intellisafe-autopilot/C26

178 Gatersleben, B. et al 2013, Hoody, Goody or Buddy? How Travel Mode Affects Social Perceptions in Urban Neighbourhoods

179 HBO, 2013, Oh My God Comedy Special, Louis CK

180 Mattisson K., Håkansson C,. Jakobsson K., 2015, Relationships Between Commuting and Social Capital Among Men and Women in Southern Sweden, Environment and Behavior

181 Wikipedia, 2015, http://sv.wikipedia.org/wiki/F procentC3 procentA5ngarnas_dilemma

182 Stockholm Direkt, 2015, Swedenborgsgatan blir gågata i sommar – bilister inte så peppade, http://www.stockholmdirekt.se/nyheter/swedenborgsgatan-blir-gagata

183 Survey conducted by Happy Sweden and Stipo in the summer of 2015.

184 Wikipedia, 2015, https://en.wikipedia.org/wiki/Free_rider_problem

185 Explorable, 2015, Choice Blindness, https://explorable.com/choice-blindness

186 World Resources Institute, 2015, Cities Safer By Design

187 Ingraham, C, 2015, Guns Are Now Killing as Many People as Cars in the US, The Washington Post, 17 dec 2015

188 https://www.psychologytoday.com/blog/logical-take/201302/guns-don-t-kill-people-people-do

189 Eddie Izzard, 1999, Dressed to kill

190 Dingus, T.A et al, 2016, Driver crash risk factors and prevalence evaluation using naturalistic driving data, Proceedings of the National Academy of Sciences of the United States of America, vol 113 no 10

191 From an interview with Caroline Samponaro at a Manhattan café in the summer of 2015

192 www.crashnotaccident.com

193 Interview with Mike Lydon conducted underneath Brooklyn Bridge near his office in the DUMBO district, New York, summer 2015

194 Schwartz, S.L., 2016, Street Smart: The Rise of Cities and the Fall of Cars

195 Montgomery, C. 2012, Happy City

196 http://www.alternativstad.nu/

197 http://www.alternativstad.nu/

198 Stahre, U, 1999, Den alternativa staden

199 Wikipedia, 2015, https://en.wikipedia.org/wiki/Provo_(movement)

200 Stahre, U, 1999, Alternativa staden: Stockholms stadsomvandling och byalagsrörelsen

201 Planka.nu, 2011, Trafikmaktordningen

202 Planka.nu, 19/12 2014, Läs talet från demonstrationen mot massbilism, https://planka.nu/2014/12/19/las-talet-fran-demonstrationen-mot-massbilism/

203 Wikipedia, 2015, http://sv.wikipedia.org/wiki/Reclaim_the_City

204 Lydon, M. & Garcia, A. 2015, Tactical Urbanism: Short-term Action for Long-term Change

205 Lydon, M. & Garcia, A. 2015, Tactical Urbanism: Short-term Action for Long-term Change

206 Green Guerillas, http://www.greenguerillas.org/

207 Trädgård på spåret, http://pasparet.org/

208 Johansson, S. C. W. & Österlin, C., 29/5 2015, Lagrummet: Allt går med fyra hjul, Archileaks, http://archileaks.se/redaktionellt/lagrummet/

209 http://parkingday.org/

210 Open Streets Project, http://openstreetsproject.org/

211 Wikipedia, 2015, https://sv.wikipedia.org/wiki/I_stan_utan_min_bil

212 European Mobility Week, 2015, http://www.mobilityweek.eu/

213 European Mobility Week, 2015, Participation Report 2015

214 Car Free Regent Street Every Sunday in July, Evening Standard, 11/6, 2013

215 Janette Sadik-Khan, https://www.ted.com/talks/janette_sadik_khan_new_york_s_streets_not_so_mean_any_more

216 Lydon & Garcia, 2015, Tactical Urbanism: Short-term Action for Long-term Change

217 Lydon & Garcia, 2015, Tactical Urbanism: Short-term Action for Long-term Change

218 New York City DOT, 2008, World Class Streets

219 Project for Public Spaces, 2015, Bryant Park, http://www.pps.org/projects/bryantpark/

220 http://www.pps.org/reference/wwhyte/

221 Andersson, O. 2012, Vykort från Utopia

222 Statens planverk, 1968, Riktlinjer för stadsplanering med hänsyn till trafiksäkerhet: Scaft 68

223 Andersson, O. 2012, Vykort från Utopia

224 Janette Sadik-Khan, https://twitter.com/JSadik-Khan

225 Bevilacqua, M., 5/4 2012, INTERVIEW: John Norquist and Our Congestion Obsession, Next City, https://nextcity.org/daily/entry/interview-john-norquist-and-our-congestion-obsession

226 Sadik-Khan, J. & Solomonow, S, 2016, Streetfight: Handbook for an Urban Revolution

227 Trafikverket, 2015, Förbifart Stockholm, http://www.trafikverket.se/forbifartstockholm

228 Klimatpartier, 2015, Så här har vi räknat, http://klimatpartiet.se/sa-har-har-vi-raknat/

229 Wikipedia, 2015, https://sv.wikipedia.org/wiki/S%C3%B6dergatan,_Stockholm

230 NACTO, 2013, Urban Street Design Guide

231 Wikipedia, 2015, https://en.wikipedia.org/wiki/Induced_demand

232 Jaffe, E., 11/11 2015, California's DOT Admits That More Roads Mean More Traffic, Citylab, http://www.citylab.com/commute/2015/11/californias-dot-admits-that-more-roads-mean-more-traffic/415245

233 Schwartz, S.L. 2015, Street Smart: The Rise of Cities and the Fall of Cars

234 Schiller, P. 2010, An Introduction to Sustainable Transportation

235 Norquist, J., 15/12 2011, The Case for Congestion, Citylab, http://www.citylab.com/commute/2011/12/case-congestion/717/

236 NACTO, 2015, Urban Street Design Guide, http://nacto.org/publication/urban-street-design-guide/

237 Janette Sadik-Khan, https://www.ted.com/talks/janette_sadik_khan_new_york_s_streets_not_so_mean_any_more

238 Gehl, J, 1987, Livet mellan husen; Gehl, J, 1996, Public Spaces and Public Life; Gehl, J, 2010, Cities for People

239 Project for Public Spaces, 2015, Jan Gehl, http://www.pps.org/reference/jgehl/

240 Speck, J, 2013, Walkable City – How Downtown Can Save America One Step at A Time

241 Speck, J, 2012, The Walkable City

242 Stockholms stad, 2012, Framkomlighetsstrategin

243 http://www.muenchen.de/

244 ITDP, 2011, Europe's Parking U-Turn: From Accommodation to Regulation

245 Willsher, K., 3/10 2015, Paris's First Attempt at Car-free Day Brings Big Drop in Air and Noise Pollution, The Guardian, http://www.theguardian.com/world/2015/oct/03/pariss-first-attempt-at-car-free-day-brings-big-drop-in-air-and-noise-pollution

246 L'Express, 5/5/2015

247 20 Minutes 22/6/2015

248 France-Presse, A., 19/10 2015, Oslo Moves to Ban Cars From City Centre Within Four Years, The Guardian, http://www.theguardian.com/

environment/2015/oct/19/oslo-moves-to-ban-cars-from-city-centre-within-four-years?C-MP=twt_a-environment_b-gdneco

249 Löken, A., 1/9 2015, Oslos nye sykkelplan: 260 kilometer sykkelvei innen 2025, Osloby, http://www.osloby.no/nyheter/sykkelpatruljen/Oslos-nye-sykkelplan-260-kilometer-sykkelvei-innen-2025-8146159.html

250 Sullivan, F., 4/12 2013, Madrid's Big Plan to Swear Off Cars, Citylab, http://www.citylab.com/commute/2013/12/madrids-big-plan-swear-cars/7744/

251 Sullivan, F., 23/2 2015, How Plans to Pedestrianize Brussels May Actually Encourage Driving, Citylab, http://www.citylab.com/politics/2015/02/plans-to-pedestrianize-brussels-encourage-driving/385753/

252 Sullivan, F., 13/7 2015, The Plan to Pedestrianize Central Milan, Citylab, http://www.citylab.com/commute/2015/07/the-plan-to-pedestrianize-central-milan/398387/

253 Sullivan, F., 16/6 2015, A Car-Free Future for Central Dublin, Citylab, .http://www.citylab.com/commute/2015/06/car-free-future-central-dublin/395969/

254 Transport for London, 2015, Travel in London, Report 8

255 Hill, D., 28/1 2016, How Would London's Next Mayor Pedestrianise Oxford Street?, The Guardian

256 Jonas Eliasson, 2012, How to Solve Traffic Jams, Ted Talk, https://www.ted.com/talks/jonas_eliasson_how_to_solve_traffic_jams

257 Valente, M., 4/3 2014, How Buenos Aires Unclogged Its Most Iconic Street, Citylab, http://www.citylab.com/commute/2014/03/how-buenos-aires-unclogged-its-most-iconic-street/8549/

258 ITDP, 7/7 2014, New São Paulo Master Plan Promotes Sustainable Growth, Eliminates Parking Minimums Citywide, https://www.itdp.org/new-sao-paulo-master-plan-promotes-sustainable-growth-eliminates-parking-minimums-citywide-2/

259 Mead, N., 11/11 2015, Viva la Revolución: Mexico City Cyclists Fight for the Right to Ride in Safety, The Guardian, http://www.theguardian.com/cities/2015/nov/11/viva-la-revolucion-mexico-city-cyclists-fight-right-safety

260 City of Helsinki, 2015, City Plan Draft Shows How Helsinki is Envisioned to Grow, http://www.hel.fi/www/uutiset/en/kaupunkisuunnitteluvirasto/city-plan

261 Helsinki Times, 4/7 2014

262 McKinsey&Company, 2015, Urban Mobility at a Tipping Point

263 McKinsey&Company, 2015, Urban Mobility at a Tipping Point

264 Goddin, P., 18/8 2015, Uber's Plan for Self-Driving Cars Bigger Than Its Taxi Disruption, Mobility Lab, http://mobilitylab.org/2015/08/18/ubers-plan-for-self-driving-cars-bigger-than-its-taxi-disruption/

265 Barter, P., 22/2 2013, Cars are parked 95% of the time. Let's Check!, Reinventing Parking, http://www.reinventingparking.org/2013/02/cars-are-parked-95-of-time-lets-check.html

266 Dan Ammann, MD General Motors http://www.wired.com/2016/01/the-metastructure-transportation

267 Goddin, P., 18/8 2015, Uber's Plan for

Self-Driving Cars Bigger Than Its Taxi
Disruption, Mobility Lab, http://mobilitylab.
org/2015/08/18/ubers-plan-for-self-driving-
cars-bigger-than-its-taxi-disruption/

268 International Transport Forum, 2015, Urban
Mobility System Upgrade: How Shared
Self-driving Cars Could Change City Traffic

269 Trafikanalys, 2015, Självkörande bilar: utveckling och möjliga effekter

270 Woodruff, M., 6/2 2015, Truck Driving
May be America's Most Popular Job, Yahoo
Finance, http://finance.yahoo.com/news/
truck-driving-may-be-america-s-most-popular-
job--182859840.html

271 Dockrill, P., 7/8 2015, Self-driving Trucks
Could Cost as Many as 7 Million Jobs in
the US Alone, Science Alert, http://www.
sciencealert.com/self-driving-trucks-could-cost-
as-many-as-7-million-jobs-in-the-us-alone

272 RT, 12/7 2014, World's First Climate-controlled Domed City to be Built in Dubai,
https://www.rt.com/news/172340-dubai-cli-
mate-controlled-city/

273 Leinberger, C, 2014, Foot Traffic Ahead

274 Leinberger, C, 2014, Foot Traffic Ahead

275 Leinberger, C, 2014, Foot Traffic Ahead

276 Leinberger, C, 2014, Foot Traffic Ahead

277 UN Habitat, 2014, The Economics of Urban
Form: A Literature Review

278 UN Habitat, 2014, The Economics of Urban
Form: A Literature Review

279 Bank of America et al, 1994, Beyond Sprawl:
New Patterns of Growth to Fit the New California

280 CEO for Cities, 2009, Walking the Walk

281 CEO for Cities, 2009, Walking the Walk

282 TMR, 2011, Värdering av stadskvaliteter

283 The University of Copenhagen & Spacescape,
2013, Værdisætning af bykvaliteter: fra hoveds-
tad til provins, IFRO Rapport 216a

284 Oldenburg, L., 4/2 2013, Stockholm växer
snabbast i Europa, Metro, http://www.metro.
se/nyheter/stockholm-vaxer-snabbast-i-europa/
EVHmbd!aRYkyk2Xjnsno/

285 William Whyte, www.pps.org

286 Interview with Tim Tompkins, New York, 2015

287 Paul Steely White i Grynbaum, M. &
Flegenheimer, M., 20/8 2015, Mayor de Blasio
Raises, Prospect of Removing, Times Square
Pedestrian Plazas, The New York Times, http://
www.nytimes.com/2015/08/21/nyregion/
mayor-de-blasio-raises-prospect-of-remov-
ing-times-square-pedestrian-plazas.html

288 PPS, 21/8 2015, Times Square Debate Lays
Bare the Importance of Proactive Public Space
Management, http://www.pps.org/blog/times-
square-debate-lays-bare-the-importance-of-pro-
active-public-space-management/

289 Davidson, J., 20/8 2015, De Blasio's Proposal
to Destroy Pedestrian Times Square Is the
Opposite of Progressive, New York Magazine,
http://nymag.com/daily/intelligencer/2015/08/
de-blasio-times-square-progressive.html

290 Tim Tompkins in Kimmelman, M., 21/8 2015,
Challenging Mayor de Blasio Over Times
Square Plazas, The New York Times, http://
www.nytimes.com/2015/08/22/arts/design/
challenging-mayor-de-blasio-over-times-square-
plazas.html?_r=0

291 PUMA, 2014, P.U.M.A.'s Top 10 Global
Trends Affecting Downtown & How to Re-
spond at Home

292 Brad Segal, PUMA

293 Montgomery, C., 2015, The Happy City Experiment, Ted Talk, http://tedxtalks.ted.com/video/The-Happy-City-Experiment-%7C-Cha

294 Bil Sweden, 2015, Utan bilen stannar Sverige, http://www.utanbilenstannarsverige.se/

295 Haglund, F., 10/12 2014, Bilen kung i EU-länderna, europaportalen.se, http://www.europaportalen.se/2014/12/bilen-kung-i-eu-landerna?utm_source=apsis-anp-3&utm_medium=email&utm_content=unspecified&utm_campaign=unspecified

296 Newman, P & Kenworthy, J, 2015, The End of Automobile Dependence: How Cities are Moving Beyond Car-based Planning

297 The Global Commission on the Economy and Climate, 2014, The New Climate Economy

298 Trafikverket, 2015, Prognos för persontransorter 2030

299 International Transport Forum, 2015, Urban Mobility System Upgrade: How Shared Self-driving Cars Could Change City Traffic

300 Mike Duggan i Smith, H., 9/1 2015, Even Detroit is Hatin on Freeways Now, Grist, http://grist.org/cities/even-detroit-is-hatin-on-freeways-now/

301 Betsy Hodges, https://twitter.com/brenttoderian/status/547514182644424705

302 Miguel Ángel at the Transforming Transportation conference in 2015, organised by the World Bank in Washington DC

303 Shankar Aggarwal at the Transforming Transportation conference in 2015

304 Anne Hidalgo i Hume, C., 10/1 2016, Mayor of Paris remains Committed to the Struggle to Reclaim Her City from the Car, The Star, http://www.thestar.com/news/gta/2016/01/10/mayor-of-paris-remains-committed-to-the-struggle-to-reclaim-her-city-from-the-car-hume.html

305 Michael Bloomberg at the Designing Cities conference in New York, 2014

306 Boston University, 2015, Menino Survey of Mayors

307 Aspen Ideas Festival 2014

308 Jaffe, E., 13/5 2015, Debunking the Myth That Only Drivers Pay for Roads, Citylab, http://www.citylab.com/commute/2015/05/debunking-the-myth-that-only-drivers-pay-for-roads/393134/

309 Wirten, P, 2012, Där jag kommer från: Kriget mot förorten

310 http://tvarstaden.blogspot.se/

311 SvD Brännpunkt 15 oktober 2008

312 SvD Brännpunkt 14 juli 2014

313 Ljunggren, S-B, 2014, Ideologier

314 Andersson, O, 2012, Vykort från Utopia

315 Svenska Dagbladet, Debatt, 17 juli 2014

316 Wall, R., 17/8 2015, "SD säger nej till förtätningen av Stockholm", DN Debatt, http://www.dn.se/debatt/repliker/sd-sager-nej-till-fortatningen-av-stockholm/

317 Nordblom, C. & Linder, C. H., 20/8 2015, MUF Stockholm: Är gatan till för bilar eller för människor? Nyheter24, http://nyheter24.se/debatt/807412-muf-stockholm-ar-gatan-till-for-bilar-eller-manniskor

318 ETC, 6/7 2015

319 www.pps.org

320 Enrique Peñalosa at the Skanska seminar at Almedalen in 2013

321 Conversation with Enrique Peñalosa, Stock-

holm, 2013.

322 Montgomery C, 2013, Happy City

323 Harvey, D., 2008, The Right To The City, New
     Left Review 53

324 Lefebvre H, 1968, Staden som rättighet

325 Kyte, R, 2013, City Transport: It's About
     Moving People, Not Vehicles, http://blogs.
     worldbank.org/voices/city-transit-it-s-about-
     moving-people-not-vehicles

326 Clos, J., 10/1 2014, Compact Cities to Address
     Climate Change, Climate Action Programme,
     http://www.climateactionprogramme.org/
     climate-leader-papers/compact_cities_to_ad-
     dress_climate_change

327 Filipe Calderon at the Transforming Transpor-
     tation conference, 2015

328 Clos, J., 10/1 2014, Compact Cities to
     Address Climate Change, Climate Action Pro-
     gramme, http://www.climateactionprogramme.
     org/climate-leader-papers/compact_cities_to_
     address_climate_change

329 Clos, J., 10/1 2014, Compact Cities to
     Address Climate Change, Climate Action
     Programme, http://www.climateactionpro-
     gramme.org/climate-leader-papers/compact_
     cities_to_address_climate_change

330 Clos, J., 10/1 2014, Compact Cities to
     Address Climate Change, Climate Action Pro-
     gramme, http://www.climateactionprogramme.
     org/climate-leader-papers/compact_cities_to_
     address_climate_change

331 Filipe Calderon at the World Urban Forum in
     Davos, 2015

332 The Global Commission on the Economy and
     Climate, 2015, The New Climate Economy,
     http://newclimateeconomy.net/

333 The Global Commission on the Economy and
     Climate, 2015, The New Climate Economy,
     http://newclimateeconomy.net/

334 The Global Commission on the Economy and
     Climate, 2015, The New Climate Economy,
     http://newclimateeconomy.net/

335 Thorpe, D., 2/2 2015, Can We Design Cities
     That Don't Need Cars?, World Economic
     Forum, https://agenda.weforum.org/2015/02/
     can-we-design-cities-that-dont-need-cars/

336 WWF, 2015, We Love Cites, http://www.
     welovecities.org/

337 Sierra Club, 2015, Sprawl overview, http://
     vault.sierraclub.org/sprawl/overview/

338 EPA, 2015, National Award for Smart Growth
     Achievement, http://www2.epa.gov/smart-
     growth/national-award-smart-growth-achieve-
     ment

339 Naturskyddsföreningen Stockholms Län, 2011,
     Policy för hållbar stadsutveckling

340 Encyclical Letter Laudato Si' of The Holy Fa-
     ther Francis on Care for Our Common Home
     (https://laudatosi.com)

341 Encyclical Letter Laudato Si' of The Holy Fa-
     ther Francis on Care for Our Common Home
     (https://laudatosi.com)

342 Encyclical Letter Laudato Si' of The Holy Fa-
     ther Francis on Care for Our Common Home
     (https://laudatosi.com)

343 Encyclical Letter Laudato Si' of The Holy Fa-
     ther Francis on Care for Our Common Home
     (https://laudatosi.com)

344 United Nations (UN), 2014. World Urban-
     ization Prospects, the 2014 revision. UN
     Department of Economic and Social Affairs,
     Population Division.

345 Floater, G. et al., 2014, Cities and the New Climate Economy

346 Glaeser, E, 2011, Triumph of the City: How Our Greatest Invention Makes Us Richer, Smarter, Greener, Healthier and Happier

347 DN Stockholm, 12 mars 2015

348 http://www.dn.se/sthlm/vykort-fran-framtidens-stad/

349 255 individual votes at the SR P3 web site, http://sverigesradio.se/sida/artikel.aspx?programid=2024&artikel=6265524

350 FFI Conference at Berns Conference Centre, November 24, 2015

351 The talk and poll were conducted by Spacescape's Tobias Nordström

352 Helsingborgs stad, 2014, Trafikprogram för Helsingborg

353 According to the urban developer and economist Charlotta Mellander.

354 Talk at the Future Cities summit in Dubai, 2015.

355 White & Spacescape, 2016, Urbana stråk: studie av Nynäsvägen och Örbyleden

356 Washington State Department of Transportation, 2015, Corridor Capacity Report 2015

357 Jonas Eliasson, 2012, How to Solve Traffic Jams, Ted Talk, https://www.ted.com/talks/jonas_eliasson_how_to_solve_traffic_jams

358 Ståhle, A, 2008, More Green Space in a Denser City, Urban Design International

359 Janette Sadik-Khan in Maone, A., 2012, Janette Sadik-Khan: Making a Sustainable City, Green Source, http://greensource.construction.com/people/2012/1209-making-a-sustainable-city.asp

360 Newman, P & Kenworthy, J, 2015, The End of Automobile Dependence: How Cities are Moving Beyond Car-based Planning

361 Member of the British think tank Future Cities Catapult

362 Talk given at the Flow Festival in Helsinki in 2015

363 Johnson, B., 2015, Great Horse Manure Crisis of 1894, Historic UK, http://www.historic-uk.com/HistoryUK/HistoryofBritain/Great-Horse-Manure-Crisis-of-1894/

364 Bill Ford, http://www.wired.com/2016/01/the-metastructure-transportation

365 Townsend, A. 2013, Smart Cities: Big Data, Civic Hackers, and the Quest for a New Utopia

366 www.ibm.com/smartercities

367 Putnam, R., 2001, Bowling Alone: The Collapse and Revival of American Community

368 Podcasten Vertikala samtal, avsnitt 4, http://vertikals.se/podcast/

369 Swedish Green Building Conference 2014

370 Greider, G., 17/11 2014, Stockholm borde krympa!, Metro, http://www.metro.se/kolumner/stockholm-borde-krympa/EVHnkq!9Wu4wmMsa9eNA/

371 Statens offentliga utredningar, 2008, Flyttning och pendling i Sverige, SOU 2007:35

372 Jacobs, J, 1970, The Economy of Cities

373 Johansson, M., Tillväxten kommer på landsbygden, Miljöforskning 1/2001, http://miljoforskning.formas.se/sv/Nummer/Februari-2001/Innehall/Artiklar/Tillvaxten-kommer-pa-landsbygden/

374 Glaeser, E, 2011, Triumph of the City: How Our Greatest Invention Makes Us Richer, Smarter, Greener, Healthier, and Happier

375 Wikipedia, 2015, https://en.wikipedia.org/

wiki/Urbanization

376 Wells, K., 23/9 2014, What is a city? The Atlantic, http://www.theatlantic.com/video/index/380650/what-is-a-city/

377 Fujita, M, Krugman, P, Venables, A J, 2001, The Spatial Economy: Cities, Regions, and International Trade

378 Glaeser, E, 2011, Triumph of the City: How Our Greatest Invention Makes Us Richer, Smarter, Greener, Healthier, and Happier

379 Edward Glaeser at the Urban Age conference in London 2014.

380 Marcus, L, 2010, Spatial Capital, The Journal of Space Syntax, Vol 1, No 1

381 Boal, Frederick W. (2000). Ethnicity and Housing

382 Walker, Renee; Keane, Christopher; Burke, Jessica (2010). Disparities and Access to Healthy Food in the United States: A Review of Food Deserts Literature. Health and Place.

383 Huttman, Elizabeth D.; Blauw, Wim; Saltman, Juliet (1991). Urban Housing Segregation of Minorities in Western Europe and the United States. Durham and London.

384 Danzinger, Sheldon H.; Haveman, Robert H. (2001). Understanding Poverty. New York: Russell Sage Foundation.

385 Sharkey, Patrick (2013). Stuck in Place: Urban Neighborhoods and the End of Progress Toward Racial Equality

386 Newman, P & Kenworthy, J, 2015, The End of Automobile Dependence: How Cities are Moving Beyond Car-based Planning

387 Wikipedia, 2015, https://en.wikipedia.org/wiki/Gentrification

388 Thörn, C & Holgersson, H, 2014, Gentrifier-ing

389 Florida, R., 8/9 2015, The Complicated Link Between Gentrification and Displacement, Citylab, http://www.citylab.com/housing/2015/09/the-complicated-link-between-gentrification-and-displacement/404161/

390 Interview conducted in Stockholm in 2014.

391 For example Bokriskommittén http://www.bokriskommitten.se/, Nybyggarkommissionen http://fastighetsnytt.se/2014/02/63-forslag-till-minskad-bostadsbrist/

392 Nordström Skans O & Åslund O, 2009, Segregationen i storstäderna, SNS välfärdsrapport

393 Sennett, R. 1992, The Conscience of the Eye: The Design and Social Life of Cities

394 Fanstein, S, 2011, The Just City

395 Fastighetsnytt no. 3/2013

396 Glaeser, E, 2011, Triumph of the City: How Our Greatest Invention Makes Us Richer, Smarter, Greener, Healthier, and Happier

397 Lens, M C & Monkkonen, P, 2016, Do Strict Land Use Regulations Make Metropolitan Areas More Segregated by Income? Journal of the American Planning Association, Vol 82, Issue 1, 2016

398 Mangin, J., 2014, The New Exclusionary Zoning, Stanford Law & Policy Review, Vol 25:91

399 Capps, K., 11/3 2016, Blame Zoning, Not Tech, for San Francisco's Housing Crisis, CityLab, http://www.citylab.com/housing/2016/03/are-wealthy-neighborhoods-to-blame-for-gentrification-of-poorer-ones/473349/?utm_source=SFTwitter

400 Interview conducted in October 2015 at the Piso Piloto exhibition in Barcelona.

401 Smith, S., 29/9 2011, Does Urban Growth Have to Mean Gentrification?, Forbes, http://www.forbes.com/sites/stephensmith/2011/09/29/does-urban-growth-have-to-mean-gentrification/

402 Legeby, A., 2010, Urban Segregation and Urban Form: From Residential Segregation to Segregation in Public Space

403 Penalosa, E., 2013, Why Buses Represent Democracy in Action, Ted Talk, http://www.goodreads.com/quotes/737444-an-advanced-city-is-not-a-place-where-the-poor

404 Location Affordability Portal, http://www.locationaffordability.info/

405 Based on the 2014 average income of SEK 331,480 (ca 41 500 dollars) (www.scb.se); 34 minutes' travel time corresponds to SEK 3,895 (ca 500 dollars) per month at work and one hour corresponds to SEK 6,905 (ca 865 dollars) worth of work.